Male witches
in early modern Europe

MANCHESTER
UNIVERSITY PRESS

Male witches in early modern Europe

LARA APPS AND ANDREW GOW

Manchester University Press
Manchester and New York

distributed exclusively in the USA by Palgrave

Published by Manchester University Press
Oxford Road, Manchester M13 9NR, UK
and Room 400, 175 Fifth Avenue, New York, NY 10010, USA
www.manchesteruniversitypress.co.uk

Distributed exclusively in the USA by
Palgrave, 175 Fifth Avenue, New York,
NY 10010, USA

Distributed exclusively in Canada by
UBC Press, University of British Columbia, 2029 West Mall,
Vancouver, BC, Canada V6T 1Z2

British Library Cataloguing-in-Publication Data
A catalogue record for this book is available from the British Library

Library of Congress Calaloging-in-Publication Data applied for

ISBN   0 7190 5708 6   *hardback*
        0 7190 5709 4   *paperback*

First published 2003

10 09 08 07 06 05 04 03   10 9 8 7 6 5 4 3 2 1

Typeset in Bulmer by
D R Bungay Associates, Burghfield, Berks

Printed in Great Britain
by Bell & Bain Ltd, Glasgow

CONTENTS

FIGURES

[vi]

PREFACE AND
ACKNOWLEDGEMENTS

We started to write this book as a survey of witch-hunting; it took on a new shape as our understanding of early modern witches and witchcraft changed and expanded. Parts of this work have gone through several mutations: a Master's thesis, course materials, and various conference papers.

We have preserved early modern orthography, punctuation and syntax in quotations and titles, and provided explanations as necessary.

We should like to thank Jeremy Black, Rick Bowers, Thomas A. Brady, Jr., Linda Bridges, Angeles Espinaco-Virseda, Beth Forrest, George Frost (the PhotoShop whiz), Brad Gregory, Michael Hawkins, Johannes Heil, John Kitchen, Chris Mackay, Julian Martin, Yoshie Mitsuyoshi, Christopher Ocker, Markus Reisenleitner, Petra Seegets, Jennifer Selwyn, Dennis Sweeney, the students of History 300 (autumn term 2000) and History 615 (winter 2002), the staff of Manchester University Press, and the anonymous reader commissioned by MUP for their help, comments, constructive criticism and encouragement; and the University of Alberta and its Department of History and Classics for material support. Any errors are, of course, our own. We also thank the staff of the Bruce Peel Special Collections Library at the University of Alberta and the Houghton Library at Harvard University. Finally, our families deserve our deep gratitude for their support and patience.

INTRODUCTION

In the last quarter of the twentieth century, dozens of books and articles on witches and witchcraft were published, amounting to a sort of second witch craze. These publications addressed the topic in general and in specific times and places, witchcraft, witch-hunting, images of witches, witches in art, literature, popular culture, new religious movements, witches in the past and the present, and witches in almost every imaginable connection, with the single exception of the one topic that is most foreign and most absurd to modern readers, students and scholars alike: ideas and knowledge about witches. Of the many dozens or hundreds of modern works on witches, scarcely any have addressed the single necessary precondition for the prosecution, torture and execution of witches: the certainty, to those who did the hunting, that witches existed.

In 1997, Stuart Clark published the first monograph since the time of Jules Michelet to focus on pre-modern ideas about witches.[1] Clark takes early modern ideas about witchcraft seriously; indeed, he devotes his first chapter to the language of witchcraft and the need to take 'belief' seriously as a motivating factor. However, Clark and the scholars beginning to follow his lead have retained the language of *belief*, thus implying sceptical distance in the sense that the ideas in question, while sincerely held, were not only fallacious but also entirely subjective. We do not mean to suggest that Satan-worshipping witches actually flew across the early modern European skies. Rather, we concur with anthropologist Gilbert Lewis: 'The very word "belief" often implies, in its use, a judgement about the uncertain truth or reliability of that which has been asserted; "knowledge" does not convey the same doubt. "Knowledge" is legitimate; "belief" only questionably so.'[2] When early moderns held something to be true, they seem generally to have *known* it, and (religious) *belief*, in post-Voltairean usage, is not an adequate conceptual analogy. As Edward Muir has argued, sixteenth-century Europeans held magic and witchcraft to be real.[3] That certain early modern authors occasionally expressed doubts as to the certainty of their religious knowledge, for instance, need not be any more unsettling to the paradigm we are proposing than the readiness with which physicists admit to doubts as to the nature and workings of atomic structure: despite all such doubts, what is/was *known* about atoms or witches induces people to act in confident ways, setting off atomic bombs or burning human beings (note the similarity). When we refer to religious and ideological knowledge as belief, we are not only distancing ourselves from the content (a natural enough desire in this case), we are introducing an alien distinction between what appear to us to be different elements of early modern Europeans' world view. The language of belief in witchcraft studies betrays an anachronistic, modernist and dismissive approach to a mental universe quite different from our own. We do not understand our role as historians to include a duty to judge the veracity of past ideas. As Ian Bostridge has argued, 'historical explanation of beliefs' requires the historian to attempt to be neutral as regards their truth content.[4] We have omitted the word 'belief' from our vocabulary in order to present our subjects' ideas without undue anachronism.

Female and male witches

Research is always most exciting when the data do not quite fit the established paradigms and explanatory models. An entire body of literature, mainly by avowed feminists, has argued that witch-hunting was in essence woman-hunting, despite the fact that many of those executed for the crime of witchcraft were men (see chapter 2). Various attempts have been made to explain away this feature of witch-hunting (see chapter 1), but none will really do, in part because they cannot make sense of areas like Normandy, Estonia or Iceland, where the vast majority of witches were men. A fundamental problem with previous interpretations of male witches is that they treat their subject as anomalous, even impossible. This assumption has led to the virtual exclusion of male witches from witchcraft studies, especially from those concerned with issues of gender. We have set out in this book to make the male witch visible – to construct him as a historical subject – as a first step toward a deeper understanding of the functions and role of gender in pre-modern European witch-hunting and ideas about witches. Our focus is, necessarily, not on a discrete body of court cases, local events or a specific period; rather, we begin with a critique of the very considerable historiography, based on our readings of learned demonology, statistical evidence and certain cases drawn from wide geographical and temporal spans.

The *Malleus maleficarum*, or Hammer of Witches, is the best-known early modern work on witchcraft, infamous for its misogynist statements about women and for its argument that most witches were women. With very few exceptions, modern scholars have taken a one-dimensional view of this treatise, citing it almost exclusively to illustrate the inherent misogyny of witch-hunting. Indeed, very few other treatises are ever cited; thus, in many studies, the *Malleus maleficarum* has come to represent 'the' demonological position on women and witches. It is, therefore, an appropriate starting point for an examination of attitudes toward gender and witchcraft.

The Latin word *maleficus*, and its feminine variant *malefica*, came into common use in the fourth century CE and were used widely in the medieval and early modern periods to denote a person who committed evil deeds by means of magic.[5] *Maleficus/malefica* is often translated as 'witch'. In the title *Malleus maleficarum*, the fact that the word *maleficarum* is a feminine plural noun would seem to suggest that the authors, Dominican Inquisitors Heinrich Institoris (Kramer, Krämer) and Jacob Sprenger,[6] believed that all witches were female. In Latin, groups containing both males and females conventionally are represented by the masculine plural, even if there are more females than males in the group.

[3]

The feminine plural implies an absence of males from a group; there-fore, the use of the feminine in the title *Malleus maleficarum* suggests that all witches are female.[7]

In the text itself, however, Institoris and Sprenger use both mascu-line and feminine forms of *maleficus*. Indeed, the first line of the *Malleus* reads 'Utrum asserere maleficos esse sit a deo [*sic*] catholicum quod eius oppositum pertinaciter defendere omnino sit hereticum.'[8] (Whether it is so very orthodox to insist that there are witches, given that maintain-ing the opposite of this obstinately is wholly heretical?) Where one would expect the authors to use the feminine accusative plural *malefi-cas*, they use the masculine *maleficos*. Furthermore, there are many other references to *malefici* (masculine plural) as well as to *maleficae* (feminine plural), sometimes within the same sections of text. In several instances, the text refers plainly to male witches both as specific individuals and as a group. At first glance, it seems amazing that Institoris and Sprenger, notorious to modern scholars as the primary authors of the 'witches as women' paradigm, would write about witches in the masculine at all, let alone in their opening lines.

Almost nothing has been published on this topic in academic treat-ments of gender and witchcraft, demonology, or the *Malleus malefi-carum* itself. Indeed, male witches in general are hardly to be found in witchcraft historiography, despite the ubiquity of gender (or rather, sex) as an issue in the study of witch-hunting and ideas about witches. There is a kind of hole at the centre of witchcraft studies, to borrow an image from Robin Briggs, into which male witches and learned discourse about them have disappeared.[9] This absence is especially striking in the work of Stuart Clark, who, in an otherwise masterly analysis of early modern demonology, suggests that witchcraft theorists were incapable of conceptualising male witches. This blind spot in witchcraft histori-ography requires attention.

Of course, the historiographical gap is a common trope with which to introduce a historical study. But research ought to do more than add a little plaster to existing structures. In order to offer a real contribution, it ought to confront and challenge those structures. In the case of this project, this means confronting a historiography committed to causal explanation and to a polarised, essentialising view of gender and its relationship to witch-hunting and ideas about witches. It also means engaging with a strongly politicised discourse about witches: inside the academy and without, the female witch is a potent symbol of women's oppression by men and, rather paradoxically, of women's power.

The overtly political dimension to the study of witches in early modern Europe demands a high level of consciousness and reflexivity regarding language, representation, and meaning. Our goal in this book is to make what is hidden visible: not only male witches themselves, but also the historiographical structures and politics that exclude them as historical subjects. This may seem threatening to some readers, especially to those with a heavy investment in representing witches as essentially female, or in claiming the study of early modern witches as women's history. We disagree with these viewpoints, but we consider our work also to be a feminist history, in Joan Wallach Scott's sense: 'Feminist history . . . [is] not just an attempt to correct or supplement an incomplete record of the past but a way of critically understanding how history operates as a site of the production of gender knowledge.'[10] Though as historians we are clearly in one important (professional) sense insiders, we also consider our perspectives to be those of outsiders, and in the interest of transparency, we should like to point out that an atheist and a Jew have relatively little *personal* investment in Christian approaches to witchcraft. Our ideological and professional investments are, we trust, clearly enough articulated over the course of the book.[11]

Our concentration on male subjects may appear to subvert the feminist project of constructing women as historical subjects, or to diminish the importance of the female witch. We prefer to think of it as a logical application of a relational concept of gender, in which men and women are defined and constructed in terms of one another. Andrea Cornwall and Nancy Lindisfarne have criticised the relational concept of gender on the basis that it is too narrow to admit of possibilities other than simple male–female difference. We agree with this view, and our understanding of gender incorporates those possibilities, including hierarchical differentiation within genders. The relational concept, nevertheless, is the core of our concept of gender.[12] With this understanding of gender and its historical construction, male witches are neither irrelevant nor a threat; they are necessary components of a complex phenomenon. Any endeavour to understand the relationship between gender and witchcraft has to take male witches into account and explain how they 'fit' within the gendered framework of early modern ideas about witches; without them, we are ignoring one half of the gender relationship and, necessarily, limiting our knowledge about both men and women in early modern Europe. As Caroline Walker Bynum has put it, 'the study of gender is a study of how roles and possibilities are conceptualized; it is a study of one hundred per cent, not of only fifty-one percent, of the human race.'[13]

Willem de Blécourt has articulated a useful gender-based approach to witchcraft and witchcraft accusations in his article 'The making of the female witch: Reflections on witchcraft and gender in the early modern period'. He argues that witches were 'made' locally, except when demonic influence was adduced (as in the 'witch-panics'); and suggests that '[a] witchcraft accusation . . . articulated the crossing of male-designated boundaries rather than being restricted to a specific female space'.[14] This suggestion sees gender as embedded in and structuring social relations, rather than as a free-floating 'concept'. Steve Hindle uses gender in the same functional rather than reified way in his article on gossip, gender and authority in early modern England.[15] In both instances, the category 'gender' contributes to historical examination of women and men, female and male spheres, and their interactions with one another.

This volume is an attempt at such an explanation. Ideas about witches and a number of episodes of witch-hunting serve as windows into gender relations at an especially fraught and vexed juncture in occidental history. The book contains three main arguments: first, that male witches have been excluded from witchcraft historiography and that this exclusion by modern scholars is not congruent with early modern understandings of witches; second, that explanations of the dynamics of witchcraft prosecutions should be applied equally to both female and male witches; third, that male witches could exist within the framework of early modern ideas about witches because they were implicitly feminised. Although the first chapters focus on our disagreements with prevailing views about male witches, our conclusions are not utterly opposed to modern scholarly understandings of the relationship between gender and witchcraft. Indeed, our argument that male witches were implicitly feminised tends to support the view that early modern Europeans correlated witchcraft with women very closely. On the other hand, this correlation was neither exact nor straightforward.

We have attempted to maintain consciousness and reflexivity regarding language, representation, and meaning. The questions that propelled the first stages of this work grew out of a close reading of the *Malleus maleficarum*, and were as follows: what did Institoris and Sprenger mean when they used the masculine *malefici*? Why did they sometimes write *malefici* and sometimes *maleficae*? Were they alone in following this pattern of grammatical gendering, or was it the usual practice in early modern witchcraft treatises? Most importantly, how much significance should one attach to the language of witchcraft literature, not just to what was said but also to the ways in which things were said?

Renato Rosaldo has written that 'no mode of composition is a neutral medium'.[16] This is as true of our own writing as it is of early modern witchcraft theorists; if we ascribe significance to their language choices, then we must be aware of the significance of our own. In addition, we must be conscious that we are ascribing significance to the empirical fact that there were male witches and that witchcraft theorists discussed them. As Keith Jenkins points out, 'facts' are selected, distributed, and weighted in finished narratives: 'The facts cannot themselves indicate their significance as though it were inherent in them. To give significance to the facts an external theory of significance is always needed.'[17] In other words, meanings are made, not found. Roland Barthes has argued that creating meaning is the essence of what historians do: 'The historian is not so much a collector of facts as a collector and relater of signifiers; that is to say, he organizes them with the purpose of establishing positive meaning and filling the vacuum of pure, meaningless series.'[18] It is important, therefore, to be open about the kinds of assumptions and positions that inflect the meanings one creates.

An examination of the word 'witch' should provide a useful approach to our policy of disclosure. The term is unavoidable, but it is extremely problematic because of the range of meanings associated with it. To begin with, in modern English usage, the word 'witch' almost invariably denotes a female person, a woman or a girl. For example, the *Concise Oxford Dictionary* defines 'witch' in female terms, as 'a sorceress, esp. a woman supposed to have dealings with the Devil or evil spirits.' The Harry Potter phenomenon obliges us to comment on the word 'wizard', which was almost never used in pre-modern sources as a male synonym for witch. The root word 'wise' implies knowledge, and the term was used primarily for learned practitioners of the magical arts (*ibid.*), not for practitioners of 'diabolical sorcery'. In the *Daemonologie, in Forme of a Dialogue*, a work claimed by King James I and VI, the characters discuss the difference between *magicians* and *necromancers* on the one hand, and *sorcerers* and *witches* on the other. The former are learned men who, by virtue of a pact with the Devil, *seem* to be able to command him to perform certain acts or services for them, though in fact this is merely a ploy of his to gain possession of their soul; the latter are simple folk who are but the servants or slaves of the Devil.[19] The term 'warlock' is used commonly now to denote a male sorcerer, but this usage implies that there is some distinction between witches and warlocks. The Old English root of the word 'witch' has two forms: *wicca*, for a male witch, and *wicce* for a female. 'Warlock' is rooted in a different semantic field: 'oathbreaker, traitor, or devil'.[20] Modern English has lost the explicitly gendered forms of 'witch', and attributes the feminine gender to the word implicitly. The modern use of two different words for male and female witches is problematic because it encourages the exclusion of men from discussions about pre-modern witches and by extension, about witch-hunting.

In both Latin and French, two very common words for 'witch' are used for both men and women, the only distinction being the gender-indicative endings. In Latin, the most common word is *maleficus/malefica*; French has *sorcier/sorcière*. German has *Hexe*, a feminine noun now conventionally used to refer to female witches; early modern German used a number of variants for male witches (as opposed to learned magic users), such as *Unhold*, *Drudner* and occasionally *Hexenmeister*. There are many other terms as well, including gender-specific words such as *necromanticus* (or *nigromanticus*) and *pythonissa*, which were specialised terms for certain kinds of magic-users.[21] In general, however, early modern authors employed rather generic words when they talked about magic-users, words that did not distinguish between male and female witches as witches.[22]

The closest English equivalent to this kind of non-distinguishing language is 'sorcerer/sorceress'. In the interests of strict correspondence with early modern style, we considered using these terms instead of 'male witch' and 'female witch'. We decided against it, however, because it could lead to some confusion when discussing other scholars' work. In addition, it would mean backing off from an engagement with the various interpretations of 'the witch' when the point of the exercise is to open up debate on precisely that issue. We use 'witch' for both men and women, with the gender specified as necessary for clarification. Despite the problems of modern English usage, this is consistent with early modern categories and usage.

The second problem with the word 'witch' is more complex. To whom does the label apply? Given that for most people today, or at least most potential readers of this book, early modern witchcraft was not 'real', what does it mean to refer to a historical subject as a witch, without quotation marks around the word? The question leads directly into a thorny tangle of issues, including realism, referentiality, agency, and subjectivity. There is not enough space here to do full justice to each of these topics; nevertheless, it is important to address them and establish our positions explicitly.

In the first chapter of his book *Thinking With Demons: The Idea of Witchcraft in Early Modern Europe*, Stuart Clark tackles the problems of realism and referentiality head-on. He states that the witchcraft beliefs of the past have been assumed by modern scholars to be utterly wrong about the possibility of supernatural events occurring because scholars are generally committed to a realist epistemology, even if they do not acknowledge it. This model views language as a simple and unproblematic reflection of an outside reality and judges utterances to be true or false as measured by the accuracy of their description of objective things. Ideas about witches, for example the idea that witches flew to Sabbaths, do not, generally speaking, correspond with 'the real activities of real people'; in Clark's terms, they lack referents in the real world. According to Clark, this lack of reference to an empirical reality has led scholars to dismiss early modern ideas about witchcraft as irrational, or to explain them away as the secondary consequences of some genuinely real and determining condition: that is to say, some set of circumstances (social, political, economic, biological, psychic, or whatever) that was objectively real in itself but gave rise to objectively false beliefs. Clark objects to these two approaches on the grounds that they make it impossible to interpret witchcraft beliefs as beliefs in terms of either their particular meaning or their ability to produce concrete actions.[23]

What is needed, he argues, is a more useful (Saussurean) approach, according to which language is not constituted by reality, but rather itself constitutes reality. This understanding of language suggests that success in communicating meanings depends upon relationships within the language system, not on relationships between the system and things external to it. Were one to subscribe to this view of language, one's focus of enquiry would shift away from putative external determinants of ideas about witchcraft to the meanings of those ideas within their specific frameworks. This does not mean that the historian would have to accept pre-modern ideas about witchcraft; rather, the whole issue of the truth or falsity of those ideas would become irrelevant. As Clark puts it, 'Witchcraft's apparent lack of reality as an objective fact would simply become a non-issue, and the consequent need to reduce witchcraft beliefs to some more real aspect of experience would go away', thus freeing historians to concentrate their interpretative endeavours on the ways in which the ideas made sense to those who held them.[24]

Clark's approach to ideas about witchcraft and language provides some of the major underpinnings of this book. Our interest in male witches is precisely in elucidating how they fit into an ostensibly misogynistic framework, or, to put it another way, into an early modern web of ideas about witches, men, and women. Behind this interest lies the assumption, which we share with Clark, that ideas that survived for nearly three centuries 'must have made some kind of sense'.[25] Witchcraft 'beliefs' do not have to be true in terms of our epistemology (our 'web of beliefs') in order to have seemed rational and coherent to early modern Europeans.[26]

In regard to the labelling of early modern men and women as witches, a non-realist methodology allows one to bypass the process of deciding whether or not each individual is 'really' a witch, since there is no way of determining this outside their frame of reference. For the purposes of this enquiry into the early modern web of ideas about witches, if a person was understood as a witch in the past, then he or she was one and will be referred to as such.

This leads us to problems of subjectivity and agency. By adopting, without qualification or quotation marks, the label *witch*, we leave ourselves open to the charge that we are replicating injustices perpetrated against those accused of witchcraft. For some modern authors, those accused and executed were victims, and should be discussed as such. These authors tend also to identify with the (female) 'victims'. Anne Barstow, for instance, who employs the rhetoric of victimhood to great effect, dedicates her book *Witchcraze* to 'those who did not survive'.[27] One could argue that it is legitimate to refer to early modern witches as victims if one is interested primarily in the perspective and experiences of the accused. On the other hand, there are several problems with this approach.

First, the identification of modern feminist scholars with early modern witches seems, as Diane Purkiss has suggested, impertinent. Barstow's dedication assumes a commonality of experience with the witches, an assumption concerning which Diane Purkiss' remarks are particularly apt: 'In the face of a degree of fear and suffering which most of us cannot even imagine, a more humble and less eager identification might be advisable.'[28]

More importantly, however, the use of victimisation rhetoric introduces methodological problems. Referring to witches as victims imposes a single perspective on a multitude of actors. There is no way to employ the rhetoric of victimisation in a sweeping fashion and at the same time offer meaningful and nuanced interpretations of those who accused, tried, tortured, executed, or just wrote about witches: the frames of reference are incompatible. Indeed, it is doubtful that calling witches victims is always consistent with the perspective of the witches themselves. Diane Purkiss, Lyndal Roper, and Malcolm Gaskill have produced studies that suggest witches possessed agency and, in some cases, represented themselves as witches deliberately.[29]

Nevertheless, it is true that our adoption of witch-hunters' and witchcraft theorists' categories and views of witches objectifies to some degree the individuals caught on the receiving end of witch trials. This is regrettable, even distasteful, given the ordeals many of the witches suffered; however, it is unavoidable in a study devoted primarily to the ideas of those who thought witches were real and dangerous. There is very little room for manoeuvre on this point; either one respects historical actors' categories or one does not.

The existence of male witches, and particularly their presence in demonological treatises, raises many questions. Can the male witch be assimilated into discussions framed by ideas about patriarchal oppression? Is the male witch a figure of the earlier witch-hunting phase only? Were male and female witches believed to be fundamentally different? Were male witches somehow gendered 'female' by witchcraft theorists? How can gender theory help us make sense of the conceptual relationship between male and female witches?

We submit that the male witch was not, conceptually speaking, different from the female witch. Early modern writers refer to male witches throughout the witch-hunting period, not just at the beginning. The male witch was not feminised in the ways one might expect; that is, the male witch was not assumed to be, or normally described as, homosexual or effeminate. He was, however, connected with female witches, and femaleness, via the medieval and early modern sense that it was primarily the weak-minded (especially women) who could be duped by the Devil into becoming his servants. The male witch suggests that biological sex was not, at the conceptual level, the primary characteristic of the witch; gender was. The primary affinity between male and female individuals with witchcraft was related to their status as (womanly) 'fools'. Women were by pre-modern lights more prone to weak-mindedness, but men were by no means immune; and, like women, foolish men represented threats to the (patriarchal) social order. Male and female witches thus have more in common than the majority of participants in the witchcraft and gender debate suggest.

The reality of witches

The question 'Were there *really* witches?' might seem the most obvious and natural one to pose after encountering the grim evidence of late-medieval and early modern witch trials. Yet for the majority of early modern Europeans, there could be no serious doubt about the existence of witches, especially for those involved in laying the theoretical and legal groundwork for the prosecutions, for those who accused people of witchcraft, for those who did the torturing and executing, and probably also for those accused of witchcraft. For almost all of them, the existence of witches and of evil magic was a foregone conclusion, as self-evident as the earth's orbit around the sun is to us. They had every reason to 'believe', indeed to *know* that witches existed. Ideas about witches had been authoritative long before the witch trials of the fifteenth to the eighteenth centuries and continued to exist in Europe and Britain for some considerable time after the witchcraft laws had been repealed.[30] Yet scholars have dismissed 'belief' as a universal, a constant that explains nothing[31] and gone looking for social, economic, even biological and meteorological causes for 'witch crazes', to the point that a widespread, consistent and authoritative discourse about diabolical witchcraft is made to seem less important than the individual, quite disparate and often seemingly random triggers that sometimes unleashed a major persecution, and that sometimes had no effect at all.

The question whether or not witches *really* existed is a modern invention. It has little or nothing to do with 'actors' categories', the thought-worlds and views of late-medieval and early modern Europeans, Britons and Americans.[32] We have asked the question for a few hundred years now, ever since the witch trials ended in the eighteenth century. Scholars first answered 'No', in the rational spirit of the European 'Enlightenment', then 'Yes', in the spirit of Romantic and medievalist folklore. Since the beginning of the twentieth century, these opposing positions have defined the debate: those to whom even the idea of a witch or witchcraft is dangerous, superstitious nonsense; and those who believe that there is 'more in heaven and earth' than reason and empirical observation can ever discover, and who think that there really were people who knew themselves to be witches and who knew that they practised witchcraft. Some, such as Margaret Murray, have gone so far as to suggest that witches were members of a secret and ancient 'pagan' religion that was practised uninterruptedly all through the Middle Ages.[33] In a search for origins and legitimacy characteristic of new societies and new social and religious groups, early proponents of the modern witch-religion Wicca founded their belief system on the idea that witchcraft is an ancient religion that was suppressed for a long time, but never extinguished; though there is very little evidence, if any, for this idea.[34]

However, there is rarely a simple answer to so simple a question, as the newspaper editor was forced to admit when he answered 'Yes, Virginia, there is a Santa Claus.' Both witches and Santa Claus exist(ed) not because there really were or are people who ride around on broomsticks or in magical sleighs, but because some people think/thought these things to be true. Ideas can be more important than 'reality' – even (perhaps especially) if we concede that there is such a thing as reality outside what we perceive. It is unsettling to contemporary world views, formed by trust in science, empirical methods and experimentation, to be confronted by what seems to be nothing but 'belief', but which was firmly proven knowledge centuries ago.

Perhaps more unsettling is that there probably is a certain amount of historical 'hard fact' behind both stories. The North American Santa Claus[35] is a version of the traditional Christian figure St Nicholas (feast day: 6 December), a bishop born around 280 CE in Asia Minor who is said to have been especially generous: whence the tradition of giving presents at Christmas-time. Carlo Ginzburg has argued that European ideas about witchcraft are based on actual remnants of folk or 'pagan' religion,[36] and most historians will agree that folkloric medicine, herbal cures and traditional knowledge about the natural world helped shape what came to be dangerous ideas about diabolical witchcraft. There is (or ought to be) a large distance between recognising historical roots, or the nuggets of truth behind a legend, and thinking that the legend itself is true. If we assume that a lack of evidence is simply the result of oppression or suppression, then we must also believe in Atlantis, the extra-terrestrial origin of the pyramids, or the existence of werewolves and vampires. There are better and simpler explanations for all these notions and any underlying phenomena than their literal existence.

Historians not only study the past; we also make it. Much of what we think about witches comes from the above-mentioned traditions of Enlightenment and Romantic scholarship. To both camps, the witch provided a useful test case, a means to prove a broader set of ideas and values using an unquestionably important phase in the common western past. If pre-Enlightenment Europeans were so fatally wrong about the existence of witches, then the rest of their world view must also be suspected of the worst inconsistencies, irrationalities and errors. The project of 'enlightenment' was to prove just that, to depict an irrational *ancien régime* so decayed, so perverse and dangerous, especially to the powerless and the marginal, that only a new and rational world view could replace it. The Romantic reaction was to insist on the value of tradition, of mystical and spiritual perception and experience, especially that of the common people, putatively unspoiled by industrialisation and urbanisation; and to rescue the non-material, the numinous, from the sceptical gaze of the deists and atheists. Tenacious herbal lore or even pagan survivals were in the Romantic age not part of a decayed and intellectually bankrupt old world, but precious evidence of the value and richness of folk tradition.

Therefore, a historian's intellectual and ideological background and constitution play a strong role in determining how he or she will see both ideas about witches and the witch trials themselves. As Diane Purkiss has argued, the academic 'discourse' of historians studying witchcraft, especially in England, is essentially a male product, mainly about women, of scholars uneasy with self-consciously theoretical approaches of the sort that might illuminate gender, ideology or 'belief', who describe themselves as 'sceptical empiricists'[37] and act accordingly when confronted with other people's thought-worlds and mentalities: 'Rather than trying to understand how witch-beliefs were structured for and by the believer, historians have often bent their energies towards explaining witch-beliefs *away*.'[38]

The underlying reason for this, according to Purkiss, is that 'History' is essentially an Enlightenment discourse, one of those that 'gradually displace[d] the supernatural in the seventeenth century'[39] and thus was programmed from the start to stake out claims to truth on territory previously occupied by interpreters and practitioners of the supernatural. While many contemporary historians have engaged with the post-structuralist and postmodern challenges to 'enlightenment truth-claims', Purkiss points out that most scholars of English witchcraft have not, and the result, until quite recently, has been stagnation and conceptual constipation.[40] No new insights into witchcraft can be gained so long as it is part of a hegemonic male academic discourse that brushes off the rather different ideas and subjectivities of people who lived a long time ago under often cruel conditions.

Carlo Ginzburg has also attacked the English tradition of witchcraft studies, focusing on the naive empiricism and terminology of Keith Thomas and Alan Macfarlane, among others, whose approach to 'belief' was influenced by anthropological functionalism and thus uninterested in its symbolic dimension.[41] Ginzburg's critique of Macfarlane is harsh:

> Macfarlane examined the age and sex of those accused of witch-craft, the motives for the accusation, their relationships with neighbours and the community in general: but he did not dwell on what those men and women believed or claimed to believe. Contact with anthropology did not lead to an intrinsic analysis of the beliefs of the victims of persecution.[42]

In this book we assume that there were some people, in some times and places, who thought 1) that they were witches; and 2) that they practised (for good or for ill) magical arts. This has been demonstrated by Carlo Ginzburg, among others. However, we insist that the majority of those accused, tortured and even burned as witches did not think of themselves as such, at least not before their interrogation. They were 'made', as de Blécourt puts it, but not only by (gendered) village dynamics. That many were willing to confess to participating in the witches' Sabbath or to practising 'black arts' reflects not only the efficacy of the means of persuasion (physical and cultural), but also the predominance and widespread acceptance of ideas about witches in their environment – rather than real events, as Murray claimed. Most will have shared the idea, dominant in their societies, that witches existed, that they used magic to cause harm to people and animals, and even that they served and worshipped Satan; but they did not think, in most cases, that they themselves did so or had done so in the past, until persuaded into saying it and perhaps even believing it under extreme duress.

So the question as to the *existence* of witches and *ideas* about witchcraft is hard to separate, then as now. Most contemporary scholars do not think that those accused of witchcraft were in fact witches (or that they even understood themselves to be witches), and most also allow their readers to see that they themselves either do not 'believe' in the existence of witches and witchcraft, or consider the question irrelevant. Certain modern scholars of the witch-hunts and of witchcraft, for instance Montague Summers and Margaret Murray, have themselves thought that witches existed but held diametrically opposed views concerning the nature of witch*craft*: to Murray, it was a pre-Christian fertility religion; to Summers, a satanic cult that was the root of feminism. But the question is neither irrelevant nor clear; it is 'badly posed'.

We refuse to allow ourselves to be drawn into ideological debates between representatives of Enlightenment and Romantic ideas about the existence of witches, no matter how important they are to adherents of Wicca and similar new religions, or to agendas concerning the oppression of counter-hegemonic traditions and structures. To engage in such debates is to lose sight of the historical data and 'reality', so far as we can discern it, of witch-hunting and ideas about witches. Without such ideas, there would have been no pyres or gallows. But ideas alone are insufficient to explain the events of the period roughly 1450-1750, during which thousands of women, men and children were tortured and executed. Had ideas been enough, the fires would have been lit hundreds of years earlier and continued burning for many decades more.

Although our questions may have no general validity or answer, they are nonetheless relevant in a certain form to any study of historical events, their preconditions and their causes. Medieval and early modern westerners knew that witches and the magical arts were real; and there seems to have been a small number of people who thought either that they were witches or that they practised magic, or both. Very careful distinctions are required if we are to avoid grotesque and useless generalisations.

We offer this book not primarily as a set of original studies designed to bring to light 'new cases', nor even as a test bed to try old and established ideas by the light of new evidence. Many of these sorts of books have been published already, without the authors having stopped to consider seriously whether or not the paradigms governing their studies were leading them closer to understanding ideas about witches or witch-hunting, or even closer to understanding our culture's recent obsession with witch-hunting. Diane Purkiss has addressed the latter question usefully in her book *The Witch in History*, and we attempt the same sort of synthesis and revision of seemingly well-known sources, episodes and texts with the goal of rethinking the relationship between concepts of gender and concepts of witchcraft.

Notes

1 Stuart Clark, *Thinking With Demons: The Idea of Witchcraft in Early Modern Europe* (Oxford: Clarendon, 1999 [1997]). Jules Michelet, *Satanism and Witchcraft: A Study in Medieval Superstition*, trans. A.R. Allison (New York: Citadel, 1939; orig. *La sorcière*, Paris, 1862).

2 Gilbert Lewis, 'Magic, religion and the rationality of belief', *Companion Encyclopedia of Anthropology*, ed. Tim Ingold (London and New York: Routledge, 1994), 563–590: 565.

3 Edward Muir, *Ritual in Early Modern Europe* (Cambridge: Cambridge University Press, 1997), 216.

4 Ian Bostridge, *Witchcraft and its Transformations c.1650–c.1750* (Oxford: Clarendon, 1997), 4.

5 Fritz Graf, *Magic in the Ancient World*, trans. Franklin Philip (Cambridge, MA and London: Harvard University Press, 2000 [1997;]) orig. *Idéologie et Practique de la Magie dans l'Antiquité Gréco-Romaine*, Paris, 1994), 55. See also Edward Peters, *The Magician, the Witch, and the Law* (Philadelphia: University of Pennsylvania Press, 1992 [1978]), 154.

6 There is some debate over the actual authorship of the *Malleus*. Although Jacob Sprenger has traditionally been considered Institoris's co-author (Jean Bodin actually refers to Sprenger as the sole author of the *Malleus*), there is evidence that he had little or nothing to do with writing the book. See e.g. Hans-Christian Klöse, 'Die angebliche Mitarbeit des Dominikaners Jakob Sprenger am Hexenhammer nach einem alten

Abdinghofer Brief', *Paderbornensis Ecclesia: Beiträge zur Geschichte des Erzbistums Paderborn, Festschrift für Lorenz Kardinal Jaeger zum 80. Geburtstag am 23. September 1972*, ed. Paul-Werner Scheele (Munich: Ferdinand Schöningh, 1972), 197-205; and Peter Segl, 'Heinrich Institoris: Persönlichkeit und literarisches Werk', *Der Hexenhammer, Entstehung und Umfeld des* Malleus maleficarum *von 1487*, ed. Peter Segl (Cologne: Böhlau, 1988), 103-126. Institoris's role has not come under the same scrutiny, no doubt because his involvement in trials discussed in the text makes his authorship plain. One wonders, though: Institoris's 1485 piece on the Innsbruck trials uses feminine terminology almost exclusively, while the *Malleus* does not. Could this be an indication of multiple authorship of the *Malleus*? See Hartmann Ammann, 'Eine Vorarbeit des Heinrich Institoris für den *Malleus Maleficarum*', *Mitteilungen des Instituts für Österreichische Geschichtsforschung*, suppl. vol. VIII, ed. Oswald Redlich (Innsbruck: Wagner'sche Universitäts-Buchhandlung, 1911), 461-504. On the other hand, Segl has noted that in a later work Institoris uses the masculine genitive plural 'magorum et maleficorum': Segl, 116. See the arguments that only Institoris/Kramer was really responsible for the bulk of the text in the introduction to Heinrich Kramer (Institoris), *Der Hexenhammer. Malleus Maleficarum*. Trans. from the Latin by Wolfgang Behringer, Günter Jerouschek and Werner Tschacher, ed. and introduced by Günter Jerouschek and Wolfgang Behringer (Munich: DTV, 2001 [2nd. ed.]), 31-69. See also the opposing arguments in the forthcoming Cambridge University Press edition with a facing-page English translation of the *Malleus* by Christopher Mackay.

7 In his translation of Martin Del Rio's *Disquisitiones Magicae*, P.G. Maxwell-Stuart remarks: 'Since Latin allows a noun in its masculine form not only to stand for a masculine person/object but also to embrace both masculine and female possibilities, one is not always entitled to assume that only males are meant when, for example, the plural *malefici* appears in the text. On the other hand, one is not entitled to assume that females must be included in the intention of that particular context, either.' P.G. Maxwell-Stuart, ed. and trans., *Martin Del Rio: Investigations Into Magic* (Manchester and New York: Manchester University Press, 2000), 24.

8 Heinrich Institoris and Jacob Sprenger, *Malleus maleficarum* [1487], ed. André Schnyder (facs. edn. Göppingen: Kümmerle 1991), 7. Our translation is designed to render the form of the *quaestio* rather than its word order or grammatical morphology. We have read 'a deo' as the adverb 'adeo', along with the 1669 edition, in order to render the suggestive comparison '*so very*

orthodox' vs. '*wholly* heretical' as well as the chiastic effect of duelling opposites ('catholicum' vs. 'hereticum').

9 Robin Briggs, *Witches and Neighbors: The Social and Cultural Context of European Witchcraft* (New York: Penguin, 1998 [HarperCollins, 1996]), 10.

10 Joan Wallach Scott, *Gender and the Politics of History* (New York: Columbia University Press, 1988), 10.

11 Our other 'tribal' affiliations we consider to be of less relevance, though some are, perhaps, worth naming: Lara Apps is of mixed Baltic-British Isles ancestry, and was raised a Catholic in both eastern and western Canada; Andrew Gow is from German-Jewish, Belgian and British Isles backgrounds, was raised in French and English in Ottawa and Montreal, and is married, with two children. We both like Dr. Martens' footwear ...

12 Scott, *Gender and the Politics of History*, 29; Andrea Cornwall and Nancy Lindisfarne, 'Dislocating masculinity: Gender, power and anthropology', *Dislocating Masculinity: Comparative Ethnographies*, eds. Andrea Cornwall and Nancy Lindisfarne (London: Routledge, 1994), 11-47: 18. Gender is by no means a simple or uncontested category. While it allows us to distinguish biological from cultural or 'socially constructed' differences between male and female attributes, behaviours, expectations and attitudes, the world of gender theory is a labyrinth of conflicting ideas and interpretations. Integral to most concepts of gender is a theory of power relations that sees gender as a category of patriarchal power structures, articulated for the maintenance and justification of that relationship; see Scott, *Gender and the Politics of History*, esp. 24 and 44; for work on gender in the early modern period, see Kathleen Brown, *Good Wives, Nasty Wenches and Anxious Patriarchs* (Chapel Hill and London: University of North Carolina Press, 1996); Richard Trexler, *Sex and Conquest: Gendered Violence, Political Order, and the European Conquest of the Americas* (Ithaca, NY: Cornell University Press, 1995); Randolph Trumbach, *Sex and the Gender Revolution* (Chicago: Chicago University Press, 1998); James Grantham Turner, ed., *Sexuality and Gender in Early Modern Europe: Institutions, Texts, Images* (Cambridge: Cambridge University Press, 1995); Merry Wiesner, *Women and Gender in Early Modern Europe* (Cambridge: Cambridge University Press, 1995 [1993]). For theorising on masculinity, see, in addition to Cornwall and Lindisfarne's collection, Maurice Berger, Brian Wallis and Simon Watson, eds., *Constructing Masculinity* (New York and London: Routledge, 1995); Harry Brod, ed., *The Making of Masculinities: The New Men's Studies* (Boston: Allen & Unwin, 1987).

13 Caroline Walker Bynum, 'In praise of fragments: History in the comic mode', *Fragmentation and Redemption: Essays on Gender and the Human Body in Medieval Religion* (New York: Zone, 1992), 11-26: 17.

14 Willem de Blécourt, The making of the female witch: Reflections on witchcraft and gender in the early modern period', *Gender and History* 12, 2 (2000), 287-309: 303.

15 Steve Hindle, 'The shaming of Margaret Knowsley: Gossip, gender and the experience of authority in early modern England', *Continuity and Change* 9 (1994), 391-419.

16 Renato Rosaldo, 'After objectivism', *The Cultural Studies Reader*, ed. Simon During (London and New York: Routledge, 1993; orig. essay 1989), 104-117: 106.

17 Keith Jenkins, 'Introduction: On being open about our closures', *The Postmodern History Reader*, ed. Keith Jenkins (London and New York: Routledge, 1997), 1-35: 10.

18 Roland Barthes, 'The discourse of history', *Postmodern History Reader* (orig. essay 1967), 120-123: 121.

19 *The Concise Oxford Dictionary of Current English*, 9th edn., ed. Della Thompson (Oxford: Clarendon, 1995); *Daemonologie, in Forme of a Dialogue* [1597], ed. G.B. Harrison (New York: Barnes & Noble, 1966), 9.

20 *The Compact Edition of the Oxford English Dictionary* (Oxford: Oxford University Press, 1971).

21 Cf. the wide range of Russian terms for workers of magic. W.F. Ryan has found that the names for female practitioners of magic 'are often the etymological equivalents of names for male magicians, although a few are distinctively female only.' *The Bathhouse at Midnight: A Historical Survey of Magic and Divination in Russia*, Magic in History (University Park, PA: Pennsylvania State University Press, 1999), 85-86.

22 P.G. Maxwell-Stuart has rightly argued for a more cautious approach to translating Latin terms for workers of magic. He points out that 'the range of vocabulary in Latin to describe workers of magic is wide and yet each term is not merely a synonym of the others,' so translating each of these terms as 'witch' may be misleading. *Investigations Into Magic*, 25.

23 Clark, *Thinking With Demons*, 3-5.

24 *Ibid.*, 6.

25 *Ibid.*, viii.

26 The concept of a web of ideas is derived from Richard Rorty. Rorty treats beliefs as 'habits of action' and a web of belief as a 'self-reweaving mechanism' that reacts to the environment. Beliefs cannot be separated out from their webs: 'a belief is what it is only by virtue of its position in a web.' All

beliefs are thus already contextualised. 'Inquiry as recontextualization: An anti-dualist account of interpretation', *Objectivity, Relativism, and Truth: Philosophical Papers,* Volume 1 (Cambridge: Cambridge University Press, 1997 [1991]), 93–110: esp. 93, 98.

27 Anne Llewellyn Barstow, *Witchcraze: A New History of the European Witch Hunts* (San Francisco: Pandora, 1995 [1994]).

28 Diane Purkiss, *The Witch in History: Early Modern and Twentieth-Century Representations* (London and New York: Routledge, 1996), 13.

29 Malcolm Gaskill, 'The Devil in the shape of a man: Witchcraft, conflict and belief in Jacobean England', *Historical Research* 71, no. 175 (1998): 142–178; Purkiss, *The Witch in History,* esp. 'Self-fashioning by women: Choosing to be a witch', 145–176; Lyndal Roper, 'Witchcraft and fantasy in early modern Germany' and 'Oedipus and the Devil', *Oedipus and the Devil: Witchcraft, Sexuality and Religion in Early Modern Europe* (London and New York: Routledge, 1994), 199–225, 226–248.

30 On the continuation of both popular and learned ideas about witchcraft, see e.g. Willem de Blécourt, 'On the continuation of witchcraft', *Witchcraft in Early Modern Europe,* eds. Jonathan Barry, Marianne Hester and Gareth Roberts (Cambridge: Cambridge University Press, 1998 [1996]), 335–352; de Blécourt, 'The witch, her victim, the unwitcher and the researcher: The continued existence of traditional witchcraft', *Witchcraft and Magic in Europe: The Twentieth Century,* eds. Bengt Ankarloo and Stuart Clark (Philadelphia: University of Pennsylvania Press, 1999; London: Athlone, 1999), 141–219; Owen Davies, *Witchcraft, Magic and Culture 1736–1951* (Manchester and New York: Manchester University Press, 1999); Marijke Gijswijt-Hofstra, 'Witchcraft after the witch-trials', *Witchcraft and Magic in Europe: The Eighteenth and Nineteenth Centuries,* eds. Bengt Ankarloo and Stuart Clark (Philadelphia: University of Pennsylvania Press, 1999), 95–189; Roy Porter, 'Witchcraft and magic in enlightenment, romantic and liberal thought', *Witchcraft and Magic in Europe: The Eighteenth and Nineteenth Centuries,* 191–282.

31 E.g. Hugh Trevor-Roper, *The European Witch-Craze of the Sixteenth and Seventeenth Centuries* (repr. London: Penguin, 1990; orig. pub. in *Religion, the Reformation and Social Change,* London: Macmillan, 1967), 9.

32 See Andrew Cunningham on a similar question concerning past thought-worlds: 'To "ask" of people in the past … what their own description of their own intentional activity was, and then to take seriously what we learn (i.e., to set out to reconstruct that activity in its wholeness), is our means of "getting out of the present", or transcending our present-centredness as historians … It may turn out unfortunately for us, that what people in the

past were actually doing does not coincide with what we wanted to find them doing.' 'Getting the game right: Some plain words on the identity and invention of science', *Studies in the History and Philosophy of Science* 19 (1988), 382–383.

33 Margaret Murray, *The Witch-Cult in Western Europe* (London: Oxford University Press, 1921).

34 See Purkiss, *The Witch in History*, 30–58, for a competent if rather aggressive discussion of the origins of Wicca. For a full-length, more balanced treatment, see Ronald Hutton, *The Triumph of the Moon: A History of Modern Pagan Witchcraft* (Oxford: Oxford University Press, 1999).

35 An English version of a Dutch name (Sint (Ni)Klaas, Sinter Klaas).

36 Carlo Ginzburg, *The Night Battles: Witchcraft and Agrarian Cults in the Sixteenth and Seventeenth Centuries*, trans. John and Anne Tedeschi (London: Routledge & Kegan Paul, 1983; orig. *I Benandanti: Stregoneria e culti agrari tra Cinquecento e Seicento*, Turin, 1966).

37 Purkiss, *The Witch in History*, 60. Further, 'historians are also keen to evade belief where that is the discourse of the accused, not only because it is tainted with the scent of persecution, but also because such beliefs are as alien to the empiricism of the historian as they are to any other sort of empiricism.' (61) Purkiss is painting with an awfully broad brush here, but the outlines of her sketch convey a fairly accurate idea of its subject.

38 *Ibid.*, 61.

39 *Ibid.*

40 Besides Purkiss's own book, some complex and interesting work on English witchcraft has been published in the past few years. See e.g. Frances E. Dolan, 'Witchcraft and the threat of the familiar', *Dangerous Familiars: Representations of Domestic Crime in England 1550–1700* (Ithaca and London: Cornell University Press, 1994), 177–236; Marion Gibson, *Reading Witchcraft: Stories of Early English Witches* (London and New York: Routledge, 1999); the collection of essays in Stuart Clark, ed., *Languages of Witchcraft: Narrative, Ideology and Meaning in Early Modern Culture* (Houndmills: Macmillan, 2001 and New York: St Martin's, 2001); Diane Purkiss, 'Desire and its deformities: Fantasies of witchcraft in the English Civil War', *Journal of Medieval and Early Modern Studies* 27, 1 (1997), 103–132.

41 Carlo Ginzburg, *Ecstasies: Deciphering the Witches' Sabbath*, trans. Raymond Rosenthal (New York: Random House, 1991; orig. *Storia Notturna*, Turin, 1989), 3–6.

42 *Ibid.*, 3.

1

INVISIBLE MEN: THE HISTORIAN
AND THE MALE WITCH

Between roughly 1450 and 1750, secular, Inquisitorial, and ecclesiastical courts across continental Europe, the British Isles, and the American colonies tried approximately 110,000 people for the crime of witchcraft, executing around 60,000.[1] All historiography dealing with early modern witchcraft is concerned, on some level, with explaining why this happened. There is no shortage of interpretations: the last thirty years have seen the historical study of witchcraft transformed 'from an esoteric byway into a regular concern of social, religious and intellectual historians' who have carried out intensive, often interdisciplinary research in the archives of continental Europe, the British Isles, and the New World.[2]

This mass of research has produced a variety of explanations for the so-called witch craze, including, but not limited to: the acculturation of the masses by the elite;[3] state-building;[4] and mass psychosis.[5] One of the most contentious sets of interpretations concerns the relationship between witch-hunting and gender. Of the thousands of people tried and executed for the crime of witchcraft, 75 to 80 per cent were women. This distinctive feature of early modern witch-hunting aroused little scholarly comment until witchcraft studies entered their 'golden age' during the last quarter of the twentieth century; over time, however, the preponderance of women in this grim count has generated a complex, politicised debate over its significance.

Much valuable work illuminates the role of early modern notions of gender in witchcraft prosecutions. Unfortunately, the debate has tended to polarise those scholars, mostly feminists, who argue that patriarchy and misogyny were primary causes of witch-hunting, and those scholars who resist feminist theories and interpretations.[6] The female witch has become a site for struggles over historical method and feminist politics, but there is very little room in the research agenda for the male witch, even though men comprised 20 to 25 per cent of the total number of executed witches. What work there is on male witches tends to be limited, for the most part, to enumeration. Rigorous application of gender analysis to the male witch has so far been absent from the historiography.[7]

The exclusion of male witches from witchcraft historiography is the result of active processes and assumptions. With few exceptions, modern scholars see the witch as essentially female, and are not prepared to recognise male witches as valid historical subjects of the same importance as female witches. It is not that they are unaware of the existence of male witches. Most serious studies, including current surveys, mention male witches; however, the male witch vanishes quickly from view, as he is made invisible by a combination of rhetorical strategies. This exclusion, which inverts the elision of women from traditional history, is not restricted to feminist scholarship. Male scholars participate in the exclusion also – even when they present research that is specifically about male witches.

The debate itself is embedded within a strongly gendered discourse. For instance, it has become practically *de rigueur* to begin a 'serious' discussion of gender and witchcraft by skewering the most extreme examples of feminist interpretation one can find. The usual suspects are Margaret Murray, Andrea Dworkin, Mary Daly, Barbara Ehrenreich and Deirdre English.[8] Diane Purkiss describes this process as a 'ritual slaughter' or rite of distantiation designed to keep the academic's masculine rationality at a safe distance from feminine irrationality and credulity.[9] The kind of language that is often used supports her critique: for example, it is surely no accident that Robin Briggs refers in a conceptually insular fashion to 'the wilder shores of the feminist and witch-cult movements'.[10] His description characterises feminists and modern pagans as irrational and uncivilised Others with whom Briggs does not wish to be identified. Even though he is referring specifically to the extreme positions, it is not a great leap to associate all members of the feminist and pagan movements with 'wilder shores', and thus to discredit them by implication. Claims to occupy a middle ground often revolve around a false doxon, the purpose of which is to create an illusion of cautious moderation.

For their part, feminist scholars are eager to point out male academics' insensitivity to women and to gender issues. H.R. Trevor-Roper, Erik Midelfort, Alan Macfarlane and Keith Thomas have all been criticised for their interpretations of women as witches and witch-hunting, which implied at certain points that women were at fault. Trevor-Roper, for instance, wrote in a striking passage that

> The Devil with his nightly visits, his *succubi* and *incubi*, his solemn pact which promised new power to gratify social and personal revenge, became 'subjective reality' to hysterical women in a harsh rural world or in artificial communities – in ill-regulated nunneries ... or in special regions like the Pays de Labourd, where ... the fishermen's wives were left deserted for months. And because separate persons attached their illusions to the same imaginary pattern, they made that pattern real to others.[11]

Here we have irrational women, improperly controlled by men, as the cause of the witch-hunts.[12] This is Trevor-Roper's most detailed comment on the issue of women as witches. Erik Midelfort, writing about south-western Germany, devoted several pages to a discussion of why 'witch panics almost always singled out adult women for special attention.' He focused on demographic explanations, but remarked that 'women seemed somehow to provoke an intense misogyny at times' and that scapegoated groups attract to themselves the scapegoating mechanism.[13]

Alan Macfarlane and Keith Thomas, historians of witchcraft in England, also suggested that it was women's behaviour that caused suspicion to fall on them; however, they are criticised more often by feminists for denying a role for male–female conflict in witch-hunting. Thomas, for instance, stated that 'the idea that witch-prosecutions reflected a war between the sexes must be discounted, not least because the victims and witnesses were themselves as likely to be women as men'.[14]

Anne Barstow's views on these historians indicate the potential for polarisation between feminist and non-feminist accounts:

> Historians were denying that misogyny and patriarchy are valid historical categories and were refusing to treat women as a recognizable historical group. Reading these works is like reading accounts of the Nazi holocaust in which everyone would agree that the majority of victims were Jewish, but no one would mention anti-Semitism or the history of violent persecution against Jews, thereby implying that it was 'natural' for Jews to be victims. Without mention of a tradition of oppression of women, the implication for the sixteenth century is that of course women would be attacked – and that it must somehow have been their fault.[15]

Although Trevor-Roper, Midelfort, Macfarlane and Thomas were sympathetic generally toward early modern witches, Barstow casts these scholars in the role of Holocaust deniers and, by implication, Nazi sympathisers. She is correct to point out these historians' tendency to find fault with women's behaviour; however, her characterisation, like Briggs' description of feminists, asserts the apostolic authority of her own approach and, it could be argued, suggests that the non-feminist historians are irrational.[16]

Given the struggle for control over discourse about the female witch, one would expect to see something similar in connection with the male witch, but this is not the case. Male witches serve a useful function as spoilers of the more simplistic 'witch-hunting as woman-hunting' interpretations, but otherwise no one says much about them. Most of what is written about male witches stems directly from the conclusions drawn by Alan Macfarlane, Erik Midelfort and William Monter in their early studies of Essex, southwestern Germany and the French-Swiss border region.[17] These conclusions may be summarised as follows: a few men were accused of witchcraft, but they were usually related to a female suspect (Macfarlane); men were accused of witchcraft, sometimes in large numbers, but this happened only when a witch-hunt spiralled into a mass panic and the normal stereotype of the female witch broke down (Midelfort); men were accused of witchcraft, sometimes in large numbers, but this was because they lived in areas that conceptualised witchcraft as heresy (Monter).

Feminist and other scholars alike have quietly, sometimes silently, incorporated Macfarlane's, Midelfort's and Monter's brief remarks into their own interpretations of witchcraft and gender. This commonality is possible because of a tacit agreement that male witches are neither as interesting nor as important as female witches and, furthermore, that they are not 'proper' witches. At the extreme, this attitude toward male witches is manifested in their simple erasure from analyses of witchcraft.

An essay by the medievalist Kathleen Biddick illustrates this erasure. In her discussion of Carlo Ginzburg's book *Ecstasies: Deciphering the Witches' Sabbath*, she summarises his argument as follows:

> For him, Inquisitorial persecution and popular notions of conspiracy are serial phenomena running in a kind of zigzag way from lepers to Jews to *women* over the fourteenth century. ... In his study of the witches' Sabbath, Ginzburg divided the possibilities for continuity and discontinuity among Jews and *women* in interesting ways. Jews seem to 'disappear' from the European imaginary, and *women* almost magically take their place [italics added].[18]

This would not be an inaccurate synopsis, except that Biddick has substituted 'women' for 'witches'. Ginzburg, unusually for witchcraft historians, always refers to both male and female witches. His scheme for the shifting targets of persecuting impulses is not 'lepers to Jews to women', but 'lepers–Jews; Jews; Jews–witches.'[19]

It is difficult to imagine how Biddick could have missed Ginzburg's point that witches were, and were understood to be, both male and female. The very first words of the book are: 'Male and female witches met at night'.[20] In the chapter Biddick cites, Ginzburg says at one point that

> Like the lepers and Jews, *male and female witches* are located at the margins of the community; their conspiracy is once again inspired by an external enemy – the enemy par excellence, the Devil. Inquisitors and lay judges will search for physical proof of the pact sealed with the Devil on the bodies of the *male and female witches*: the stigma that lepers and Jews carried sewn onto their clothing [italics added].[21]

Finally, on the very page that Biddick cites from that chapter, Ginzburg remarks that 'For almost a century trials had been held against the sect of anthropophagous male and female witches'.[22] Biddick either wilfully or unconsciously eliminated the male witches, who are out in plain sight in Ginzburg's text. If she did this wilfully, distorting Ginzburg's argument along the way, it suggests a remarkable degree of arrogance; if her erasure of male witches was unconscious, it indicates that her feminist optics contain a blind spot. Either way, Biddick's inability to respect Ginzburg's sense of the term 'witch' demonstrates the power of the paradigm of the female witch and the discomfort that scholars feel when confronted with male witches.

More commonly, especially in surveys, male witches are mentioned once or twice and then forgotten, and witches are referred to subsequently as if they were exclusively female. Keith Thomas, for example, draws his readers' attention to the fact that some witches were men, but then switches to the feminine pronoun: 'A witch was a person of either sex (but more often female) who could mysteriously injure other people. The damage she might do ... could take various forms.'[23] Anne Barstow presents a particularly objectionable version of this elision. After explaining that '[i]t is through an analysis of the percentage of women and men accused and of the percentage condemned that the gender bias of this persecution emerges',[24] she goes on to say:

Given the chaotic state of the records, the temptation to round off the numbers is strong. Yet I found myself carefully retaining each awkward figure, even though this added hours of work for each region I studied. As Joan Ringelheim, researcher of women in the Nazi holocaust, stated of her work, to drop numbers now is to kill these persons twice. Wanting to record every known victim, to ensure that the historical record finally acknowledges *her* death, I offer the most complete record available at this time [italics added].[25]

Barstow envisions the dead witches as females only, even though she is well aware that thousands of men were also accused of and executed for the crime of witchcraft. According to her own standards, Barstow is killing some witches twice by speaking as if all witches were women.

One could defend Barstow's indifference toward male witches on the grounds that she is performing the important task of writing women's history. There is nothing wrong with focusing on women; however, there is something disturbing, on several levels, about an act of historiographical revenge that replicates, by inversion, the past neglect of women as historical subjects. To put the elision of male witches in perspective, one has only to read the words of Johannes Junius, who was executed as a witch in 1628. In a letter smuggled from prison, Junius wrote to his daughter

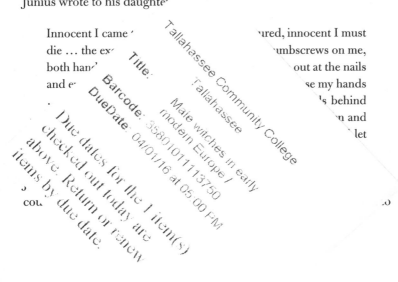

Innocent I came ... ... ured, innocent I must die ... the ex... ...umbscrews on me, both han... out at the nails and e... ...se my hands ... 's behind ...n and ... let

privilege the suffering of women over that of men. In doing so, they are committing an injustice against certain historical subjects – human beings – solely on the basis of their (male) sex.

As troubling as open exclusions are, they are less problematic than the strategies that 'declassify' male witches. Men are discussed in terms that suggest they were essentially different, as witches, from women – and therefore not really witches at all. Sometimes this approach is blunt, as in Barstow's assertion:

> The fact that overall about 20 percent of the accused were male is less an indication that men were associated with witchcraft than it appears. Most of these men were related to women already con- victed of sorcery ... and thus were not perceived as *originators* of witchcraft. Of the few who were not related, most had criminal records for other felonies ... witchcraft was not the original charge but was added on to make the initial accusation more heinous [original italics].[27]

In her survey of early modern European women and gender, Merry Wiesner presents a variation of this argument, stating that 'male sus- pects were generally relatives of the accused women' and '[t]he men accused in mass panics were generally charged with different types of witchcraft than the women – of harming things in the male domain such as horses or crops rather than killing infants or spoiling bread – and only rarely accused of actions such as night-flying or pacts with the Devil.'[28] Although Barstow and Wiesner do discuss male witches in general terms, the effect of their description is to eliminate male witches as valid historical subjects by casting them as either mere collateral damage in the persecution of women, or as something completely different from female witches and therefore uninteresting.

William Monter performs a more subtle redirection in his study of male witches in Normandy. This important article is one of the most thorough discussions of male witches, and does much to challenge the notion that early modern witch beliefs and witch-hunting were directed uniformly against women. Monter provides a wealth of data about male witches, beginning with the fact that in this 'unremarkable province' close to 'the heart of northern and western Europe', men comprised the majority of those tried and executed for witchcraft.[29] What is more, the proportion of male witches actually rose over time.[30] Finally, Monter's research indicates that certain occupational groups – shepherds, blacksmiths and clerics – were particularly vulnerable to witchcraft accusations.[31]

Monter's study of Normandy is exciting because it offers concrete evidence that early modern beliefs about witches were not necessarily sex-specific. For example, both men and women were searched for Devil's marks, with men 'as likely as women to display such anaesthetic spots.' However, Monter suggests that 'it was difficult to accommodate beliefs about the orgies at the witches' sabbath to a predominantly male population of witches'.[32] Monter does not cite any statements by the Rouen judges regarding the putative difficulty of accommodating beliefs about the Sabbath with male witches, and appears to be making a large assumption based on a relative lack of questions about the Sabbath, despite the fact that both men and women confessed to attending it.[33] According to Monter, the lack of judicial interest in the Sabbath was a means of 'finessing' the problem of men attending these witches' gatherings;[34] however, it is also possible that this indicates merely a broader disinterest in this element of witchcraft. Monter's assumption that the judges in Rouen were confused by the existence of male witches, even though they were confronted by them in relatively large numbers, suggests that it is Monter, the modern historian, who has difficulty accommodating male witches within the paradigm of early modern diabolic witchcraft.

In the end, Monter reclassifies the male witches as heretics, thus harking back to his 1976 conclusions about regions with large proportions of male witches. The Normandy witches, especially the shepherds, were in the habit of using Eucharists to perform magic. Monter argues that 'the judges of Rouen inflicted such severe punishments on those shepherds ... not because they were magicians, but because they profaned the eucharist, the body of Christ.'[35] This particular statement concerns the reason for the unusual severity of the Rouen Parlement toward male witches, not the reason for their existence in the first place; however, shortly before he makes this comment, Monter wonders 'why Normandy put mainly male witches on trial', then launches directly into his discussion of profaning the Eucharist.[36]

There is some other useful research on male witches, although it tends to be embedded in works focusing on other issues. For example, Eva Labouvie begins her article on men's roles in witch trials with a brief survey of the witchcraft literature, and takes exception to the 'unrestrained feminist nature of the arguments in witchcraft scholarship of the 1970s, which was interested only in the role of women as victims in witchcraft trials.'[37] She concentrates on the differences between the sorts of magic men and women were thought to do, thought each other did, and were accused of; the cases are from the Saarland. She also mentions the many regions of what is now Austria and Switzerland where men were the majority of the accused and lists a number of important works for these regions.[38] Labouvie notes that men were accused of certain kinds of witchcraft, mainly rooted in 'agricultural everyday reality' and male areas of responsibility (health and care of children and animals). Whereas women were accused of poisoning and 'malevolent nurture', men who used magic aimed to procure opposite effects (*Segnerei*: 'blessing'; illness-curing magic, harvest, field and weather magic; professional healing magic) may have been less likely to be suspected of diabolical witchcraft. She ends with the idea that 'the witchcraft trials that took place involving male village dwellers [in the Saarland] seem to have served in the main to regulate village power relations and conflict within the male sphere of tasks and duties, mainly within male areas of responsibility and activity'. Men were much more likely to accuse women of *maleficium* and of diabolical magic, even more than women were. Women accused men of diabolical magic, but men did not accuse other men of this; they tended to accuse men of the more traditional forms of male magic.[39] Labouvie's study suggests some intriguing avenues of investigation, especially with respect to the intersection of witchcraft accusations with gender roles; however, the overall point of the article has to do more with male participation in witch trials as accusers than with male witches.

Robin Briggs and Willem de Blécourt both have published studies that include and comment on male witches. However, Briggs concentrates on refuting the theory that witch-hunting was woman-hunting, and has little to say about male witches as witches; in his book chapter 'Men against women: the gendering of witchcraft', he focuses on female witches and accusers, and male witches play a minor role.[40] In his important article 'The making of the female witch: Reflections on witchcraft and gender in the early modern period', de Blécourt has interesting things to say about male witches in the Netherlands, including the idea that there existed both male and female witch stereotypes.[41] He raises the question of why 'the making of the male witch is as neglected as his female counterpart', but is, in this particular study, concerned primarily with the female witch. Despite his knowledge that 'in some areas men were also at risk to be socially constructed as witches', de Blécourt dismisses male witches by stating that 'their witchcraft was usually of a different, less malevolent kind and hardly susceptible to prosecution.'[42]

Stuart Clark's interpretation of demonological views of gender and witchcraft offers the most striking instance of the invisibility of male witches. Demonological literature is a major source for the assumption that witch-hunting was primarily about persecuting women. Some researchers blame witchcraft treatises, particularly the infamous *Malleus maleficarum* of 1487, for the gender bias of witch-hunts that targeted women more often than men. Gerhild Scholz Williams, for example, has written: 'Kramer's *Malleus Maleficarum* gave the starting signal to a discourse on witchcraft and women that gathered momentum in the late fifteenth and early sixteenth centuries and realized its full destructive potential between the years 1580 and 1630.'[43] Sigrid Brauner took a similar view in her study of the construction of the witch-image in early modern Germany, arguing that the *Malleus maleficarum* represented 'a watershed in the history of the witch hunts' because it marked the first time that a work on witchcraft as heresy argued that most witches were women.[44] Implicit in both of these formulations is the view that the *Malleus* was a typical demonological work: fundamentally misogynist and responsible for the high percentage of female victims of witch trials.

In his studies of early modern demonology, Stuart Clark questions both the woman-hunting argument and the attribution of blame to demonologists. He points out that if witch-hunting was indeed a function of misogyny, then 'we ought ... to find woman-hating in abundance in those who most actively supported it. The problem is that we do not.'[45] According to Clark, 'early modern demonologists showed little interest either in exploring the gender basis of witchcraft or in using it to denigrate women.' They expressed negative attitudes toward women, but these were not unusual for the time and place. This is not to say that they were not misogynists – they were – but most witchcraft theorists were not much concerned with the subject of women as witches. Drawing on a cultural heritage of ideas about women, including Aristotle's views about women as imperfect men, and the clerical misogyny of the fourteenth and fifteenth centuries, the authors of demonological treatises took women's 'greater propensity to demonism' for granted, and 'felt no need to elaborate on it or indulge in additional woman-hating to back it up.' As Clark argues, the femininity of the witch was 'more of a presupposition than a problem' for witchcraft theorists.[46]

Of course, this does not mean that misogyny had nothing to do with the association of witchcraft with women. But Clark suggests that this association operated at a fundamental conceptual level that went deeper than the social or material surface of early modern culture. He argues that a conceptual affinity between witchcraft and women made it 'literally unthinkable ... that witches should be male.'[47] This affinity derived, he argues, from the binary structure of early modern European thinking, which classified everything according to a dual symbolic system. Within this system, the male/female polarity was a primary, hierarchically weighted form of symbolic differentiation. In a nutshell, men were 'symbolically associated with a range of other positive items and categories, and women with their negative counterparts.' Rationality, for instance, a 'positive' trait associated with men, had its 'negative' counterpart, irrationality – which was associated with women. These polarised associations were not necessarily antagonistic; they were often complementary. Nevertheless, women were seen, he argues, as fundamentally negative opposites to men in all their physical, intellectual, emotional, and spiritual attributes.[48]

Witches, and witchcraft, were thought of as wholly negative, as inversions of everything good. According to Clark, their negative, inversionary 'position' within the binary cognitive framework of early modern Europe placed them, by definition, on the female side of the male/female polarity. Clark argues:

> At a demonological level ... witches were female because the representational system governing them required for its coherence a general correlation between such primary oppositions as good/evil, order/disorder, soul/body, and male/female; they were females who, by behaviour inspired by the master of inversion, the Devil, inverted the polarized attributes accorded to the genders in later medieval and early modern learned culture; and of these subversives, they were thought to be the most extreme and the most dangerous.[49]

Clark's structuralist thesis works well as an explanation of why witchcraft was generally linked with *women*; however, it does not explain why demonological treatises, like witchcraft accusations, include male witches. If the conceptual correlation between witches and women was as strong as Clark suggests, then it is very difficult to explain why early modern writers about witchcraft seemed to have no trouble imagining, discussing, and fearing male witches. Why, if the link was so clear and logical, were there any male witches at all?[50] Clark's assertion that the binary structure made it unthinkable that witches should be male simply does not correspond to the frequent references to male witches in the demonological treatises, as we demonstrate in chapter four.

Why are historians so reluctant to take male witches seriously in their analyses of gender and witchcraft? In the case of some feminist scholars, the answer is probably relatively simple: they do not consider the persecution of men to be as important as the oppression of women, and the male witch does not carry the same symbolic power for them as the female witch does. Furthermore, paying too much attention to male witches might diminish the role and significance of women in early modern witchcraft historiography. For other scholars, the male witch might represent an unwelcome link between the modern academic and the irrational. Excluding the male witch from witchcraft historiography betrays a need to distance the modern (male) academic from a witch-figure that has been constructed over time as a symbol of superstition, femininity and powerlessness. The male witch threatens this image by confusing the tidy links between femininity and witchcraft; he also threatens the self-image of the academic, who needs to represent the witch as his Other.[51] Yet others might simply be afraid of addressing the issue in print, given the assiduous polemics conducted in the commercial witchabilia industry.

We need to overcome this tendency to polarise, and to reconceptualise the nature of interlacing gendered oppositions in both modern and early modern culture. The male witch provides a means of exposing our assumptions and developing more nuanced understandings of the relationship between masculinity, femininity and witchcraft.

Notes

1 Brian Levack, *The Witch-Hunt in Early Modern Europe*, 2nd edn. (London and New York: Longman, 1995), 25. Estimates of the number of trials and executions vary, and figures such as Levack's represent a combination of hard data and 'allowances' for missing records. Levack's numbers have been accepted as reasonable, if conservative, by the general community of scholars working on this topic.

2 Robin Briggs, '"Many reasons why": Witchcraft and the problem of multiple explanation', *Witchcraft in Early Modern Europe*, 49–63: 49.

3 See e.g. Robert Muchembled, 'Satanic myths and cultural reality', *Early Modern European Witchcraft: Centres and Peripheries*, eds. Bengt Ankarloo and Gustav Henningsen (Oxford: Clarendon, 1990), 139–160.

4 See e.g. Christina Larner, *Enemies of God: The Witch Hunt in Scotland* (London: Chatto & Windus, 1981); see also Brian Levack, 'State building and witch hunting in early modern Europe', *Witchcraft in Early Modern Europe*, 96–115, for a useful discussion of this thesis.

5 See e.g. Trevor-Roper, *The European Witch-Craze*.

6 We do not mean to suggest that feminist (or non-feminist) interpretations are uniform. There is considerable range in feminist analyses, from simplistic readings of witchcraft trials as the result of unmediated male hatred of women, to sensitive and nuanced work on women's ideas about witchcraft as they related to women's identities. We have not commented in depth on most of these studies because they have little or nothing to say about male witches, though they have important things to say about female witches: see e.g. Dolan, 'Witchcraft and the threat of the familiar'; Carol F. Karlsen, *The Devil in the Shape of a Woman: Witchcraft in Colonial New England* (New York and London: W.W. Norton, 1987); Purkiss, *The Witch in History*; Roper, *Oedipus and the Devil*; Elizabeth Reis, *Damned Women: Sinners and Witches in Puritan New England* (Ithaca and London: Cornell University Press, 1999 [1997]); Deborah Willis, *Malevolent Nurture: Witch-Hunting and Maternal Power in Early Modern England* (Ithaca and London: Cornell University Press, 1995).

7 One of only a few exceptions is the excellent article by Eva Labouvie, 'Männer im Hexenprozess: Zur Sozialanthropologie eines "männlichen" Verständnisses von Magie und Hexerei', *Geschichte und Gesellschaft* 16 (1990), 56–78.

8 On Margaret Murray, see our Introduction. Andrea Dworkin is best known in the context of witchcraft studies for her claim that nine million women were burned as witches: see *Woman-Hating* (New York: Dutton, 1974). Ehrenreich and English are known for their theory that witch-hunting was a systematic attempt by male doctors to eradicate women's medicine, especially midwifery: *Witches, Midwives and Nurses: A History of Women Healers* (Old Westbury, NY: Feminist Press, 1973; London: Writers and Readers Publishing Cooperative, 1973).

9 Purkiss, *The Witch in History*, 62–63.

10 Briggs, *Witches and Neighbors*, 8.

11 Trevor-Roper, *The European Witch-Craze*, 120.

12 There can be no doubt that in early modern Europe, male honour, potency and social credit were based on ability to control 'their' women, and that whoredom, adultery and the like were often seen as perilously close to witchcraft – not least because of the implications of love magic. See Susan Dewar Amussen, *An Ordered Society: Gender and Class in Early Modern England* (Oxford: Blackwell, 1988); Brown, *Good Wives*; Elizabeth Foyster, *Manhood in Early Modern England: Honour, Sex and Marriage* (London and New York: Longman, 1999), esp. p. 66. However, this does not mean that widespread anxiety over uncontrolled women necessarily furnishes us with a general theory of witchcraft accusations.

13 H.C. Erik Midelfort, *Witch Hunting in Southwestern Germany 1562–1684: The Social and Intellectual Foundations* (Stanford: Stanford University Press, 1972), 182–183.

14 Keith Thomas, *Religion and the Decline of Magic: Studies in Popular Beliefs in Sixteenth and Seventeenth-Century England* (repr. London: Penguin, 1991 [Weidenfeld & Nicolson, 1971]), 679. Alan Macfarlane, *Witchcraft in Tudor and Stuart England: A Regional and Comparative Study* (repr. Prospect Heights, IL.: Waveland, 1991 [London: Routledge, 1970]).

15 Barstow, *Witchcraze*, 4.

16 This statement could be read another way, namely, that Barstow views non-feminist male historians as rational in a pejorative sense. This would be consistent with certain feminist theories about the link between (negative) rationality and patriarchy, as well as with interpretations of the Nazi Holocaust as a product of modernisation and rationalism. Unfortunately, Barstow does not offer a discussion of her views on rationality and Nazism. We infer, however, from her tone and her use elsewhere of expressions such as 'orgy of hatred' (*ibid.*, 54) that she interprets witch-hunting as irrational; her close association of the 'witch craze' with the Nazi Holocaust would therefore make the latter a product of irrationality also. For brief but useful discussions of Holocaust historiography, see Saul Friedländer, 'The extermination of the European Jews in historiography: Fifty years later' and Omer Bartov, 'German soldiers and the Holocaust: Historiography, research and implications', *The Holocaust: Origins, Implementation, Aftermath*, ed. Omer Bartov (London and New York: Routledge, 2000), 79–91 and 162–184.

17 Macfarlane, *Witchcraft in Tudor and Stuart England*; Midelfort, *Witch Hunting in Southwestern Germany*; E. William Monter, *Witchcraft in France and Switzerland: The Borderlands During the Reformation* (Ithaca and London: Cornell University Press, 1976).

18 Kathleen Biddick, 'The Devil's anal eye: Inquisitorial optics and ethno-
    graphic authority', *The Shock of Medievalism* (Durham and London: Duke
    University Press, 1998), 105–134: 131. Biddick's remarks about witch-
    craft are based almost entirely on a rather selective reading of the *Malleus
    maleficarum*, not, as far as we can tell, on any independent study of
    archival material. She has some interesting things to say about the con-
    struction of ethnographic authority by Inquisitors and modern microhis-
    torians; however, she offers no comment on her own reading practices or
    justification for altering the sense of Ginzburg's arguments.
19 Ginzburg, *Ecstasies*, 71.
20 *Ibid.*, 1.
21 *Ibid.*, 72.
22 *Ibid.*, 76.
23 Thomas, *Religion and the Decline of Magic*, 519.
24 Barstow, *Witchcraze*, 20.
25 *Ibid.*, 22. Given that Barstow's work is a synthesis of others' research, and
    seems to have involved no additional archival research whatsoever, her
    comment about the state of the records is misleading and self-important.
    Purkiss remarks that the appropriation of the Holocaust by radical femi-
    nists shows that 'the narrative of the Holocaust has become the paradig-
    matic narrative for understanding atrocity in the late twentieth century',
    something which, as she points out, is 'deeply problematic' as both history
    and politics. See *The Witch in History*, 16–17. Despite her clear aim to
    'debunk' the Burning Times myth of a women's holocaust, Purkiss fails to
    mention male witches.
26 Letter dated 24 July 1628. Trans. Andrew Gow. See Appendix for a more
    complete version of the letter.
27 Barstow, *Witchcraze*, 24.
28 Merry E. Wiesner, 'Witchcraft', *Women and Gender in Early Modern
    Europe*, 218–238: 233–234. Barstow and Wiesner derive their assertions
    from a combination of Macfarlane's and Midelfort's conclusions.
29 William Monter, 'Toads and eucharists: The male witches of Normandy,
    1564–1660', *French Historical Studies* 20, no. 4 (1997): 563–595: 564.
30 *Ibid.*, 584, table 3.
31 *Ibid.*, 581–584.
32 *Ibid.*, 588.
33 *Ibid.*, 589.
34 *Ibid.*, 590.
35 *Ibid.*, 592.
36 *Ibid.*, 590.

37 Labouvie, 'Männer im Hexenprozess', 58: 'die uneingschränkt feminis-
    tisch argumentierende Hexendiskussion der 70er Jahre, die auss-
    chliesslich Wert auf die Perspektive der Opferrrolle von Frauen in
    Hexenprozessen legt'.

38 H. Valentinitsch, 'Die Verfolgung von Hexen und Zauberern im
    Herzogtum Steiermark – eine Zwischenbilanz', *Hexen und Zauberer: Die
    grosse Verfolgung – ein europäisches Phänomen in der Steiermark, ed. H.
    Valentinitsch* (Graz: n.p., 1987), 297–316; P. Kamber, 'La chasse aux sor-
    ciers et aux sorcières dans le Pays de Vaud', *Revue Historique Vaudoise* 90
    (1982), 21–33; and S. Gosler, 'Hexenwahn und Hexenprozesse in
    Kärnten von der Mitte des 15. bis zum ersten Drittel des 18.
    Jahrhunderts', Diss. Graz 1955, 128–136.

39 Labouvie, 'Männer im Hexenprozess', 77–78.

40 Briggs, *Witches and Neighbors*, 257–286.

41 de Blécourt, 'The making of the female witch', 298.

42 *Ibid.*, 293.

43 Gerhild Scholz Williams, 'Magic and gender: The struggle for control in
    the witchcraft tracts of Kramer, Weyer, and Bodin', *Defining Dominion:
    The Discourses of Magic and Witchcraft in Early Modern France and
    Germany* (Ann Arbor: Michigan University Press, 1995), 65–88: 65.

44 Sigrid Brauner, *Fearless Wives and Frightened Shrews: The Construction
    of the Witch in Early Modern Germany*, ed. Robert H. Brown (Amherst:
    Massachusetts University Press, 1995), 31.

45 Clark, *Thinking With Demons*, 112.

46 *Ibid.*, 117.

47 *Ibid.*, 130.

48 *Ibid.*, 119–123.

49 *Ibid.*, 33.

50 Malcolm Gaskill poses the same question in his article 'The Devil in the
    shape of a man'.

51 We have drawn on Diane Purkiss's analysis of modern academics' rela-
    tionship to witches, *The Witch in History*, esp. 60–67.

2

SECONDARY TARGETS? MALE
WITCHES ON TRIAL

As the previous chapter showed, the prevailing view in witchcraft studies is that male witches were rare exceptions to the rule and are less important and interesting, as historical subjects, than female witches. There is a kind of conventional historiographical wisdom about male witches, which may be summarised as follows: male witches were a) accused in small numbers; b) accused primarily because they were related to female witches; c) accused primarily in large witch-hunts, in which panic broke down the stereotype of the female witch; d) not accused of diabolic witchcraft, especially the sexual aspects; e) accused in larger numbers in areas where witchcraft was treated primarily as heresy rather than as *maleficium*; f) accused of different types of witchcraft from that of female witches.

These generalisations are rarely questioned, despite the fact that they are derived, for the most part, from the early regional studies by Monter, Midelfort, and Macfarlane rather than from comparative analyses. Whereas almost everything else, it seems, about witchcraft and witch-hunting (especially anything to do with women) has been dissected under many different microscopes, these hypotheses regarding male witches, put forward in the 1970s, have been absorbed as comfortable verities and allowed to stand virtually untested.

This chapter examines cases in which men were accused of witchcraft. The examples are drawn from several different regions, in order to test conventional generalisations about male witches. Examining a few cases is not the same thing as a comprehensive comparative analysis, and one must be wary of merely replacing old generalisations with new ones; however, the examples discussed in this chapter indicate clearly that the conventional wisdom regarding male witches is faulty on empirical grounds and fails utterly to account for the complexity of witchcraft cases involving men.

As Robin Briggs has put it, 'Counting heads is a useful way of shaking our ready assumptions, and of bringing a degree of rigour into the discussion.'[1] One of the most dangerous assumptions, methodologically speaking, is to impart too much significance to the often-cited fact that women comprised 75 to 80 per cent of those tried for witchcraft in early modern Europe. This figure represents an estimate that covers continental Europe, the British Isles, and the American colonies, over a period of roughly three hundred years: it masks the crucial fact that ratios of male to female witches were extremely variable. The following table illustrates this variability between regions.

Table 1 is an original synthesis of others' archival research. Similar tables can be found in many studies. Ordinarily, they are compiled in order to marshal statistical support for arguments about witch-hunting's anti-female bias. Our purpose is different, and we have designed our table accordingly. We have omitted the usual column listing the percentage of female witches, in favour of one listing the percentage of male witches. The arrangement of data is also somewhat unusual. Instead of grouping statistics by region or chronology, we have sorted them according to an ascending numerical order of the percentages of male witches. We have done this for two reasons: first, to highlight the range of percentages; second, and more importantly, to avoid, as far as possible, giving the false impression that the data sets are directly comparable. As the second column shows, the chronological periods covered are too variable to allow a meaningful comparison of statistical data; in addition, the regions represented in this sample are very different, ranging from a city (Venice) to entire countries. Our sample is by no means intended to be exhaustive; therefore, we have not included totals. The

Table 1 *Witchcraft prosecutions by sex*[2]

Place	Dates	Female	Male	% Male
Bishopric of Basel	1571–1670	181	9	5
Hungary	1520–1777	1,482	160	10
Essex Co., England	1560–1602	158	24	13
SW Germany (executions)	pre-1627	580	88	13
New England	1620–1725	89	14	14
Scotland	1560–1709	2,208	413	16
Norway	1551–1760	c. 690	c. 173	20
SW Germany (executions)	post-1627	470	150	24
Venice	1550–1650	714	224	24
S. Sweden	1635–1754	77	25	25
Fribourg	1607–1683	103	59	36
Zeeland	1450–1729	19	11	37
Pays de Vaud	1539–1670	62	45	42
Finland	1520–1699	325	316	49
Burgundy	1580–1642	76	83	52
Estonia	1520–1729	77	116	60
Normandy	1564–1660	103	278	73
Iceland	1625–1685	10	110	92

figures include men and women who were accused, indicted or tried for witchcraft.

Although it is difficult to draw certain kinds of specific conclusions from the comparison of such diverse data sets, several features stand out. First, for a phenomenon described by one historian as the exemplification of 'men's inhumanity to women', there is a suspiciously large number of cases against men: 2,298 in this sample.[3] Second, as mentioned above, the proportion of male to female witches could be extremely varied. The statistical range from 5 per cent male witches in the Bishopric of Basel to 92 per cent in Iceland, with other regions 'filling in' the gap between those two figures, makes the value of general estimates seem highly dubious. Finally, there were regions of Europe where men actually comprised the *majority* of those accused of witchcraft: Burgundy, Estonia, Normandy and Iceland.

Perhaps we could discount Iceland and Estonia as peripheral to European culture and therefore not representative of the whole; but what about Burgundy and Normandy? In any case, it is clear that any attempt to establish representativeness would be problematic. Is the Bishopric of Basel really more representative of gendered patterns of witch-hunting than Iceland, because it tried so many more women than men? Or is Norway truly representative, on the basis of its 'perfect' number of male witches?

G.R. Quaife exemplifies scholars' difficulty in coming to grips with the fact of male witches. In his discussion of the gender bias of witch hunts, Quaife explains male witches away as the political opponents of prosecutors; as cunningmen; or as relatives of female suspects. He actually suggests that in the case of New England, the male witches who were related to a female witch 'should be discounted' in an assessment of gender bias because they were merely 'secondary targets as husbands or associates of a female witch'. Discounting these men, he argues, raises the proportion of women in the New England trials to almost 90 per cent, which, he says, corresponds neatly with the proportion in England. Quaife extrapolates from this result that 'the gender bias against women may be greater in other jurisdictions than the raw figures indicate'.[4]

In his attempt to 'improve' the proportions of accused women, Quaife fails to consider that a statistical criterion ought to be applied to an entire set of data, not to a pre-selected group only. If, as he suggests, 'secondary' targets of witchcraft accusations ought to be discounted, then the total number of witches must drop sharply. It was unusual for more than a small number of individuals to be accused as primary targets; the ordinary pattern for witch-hunts, including the New England trials, was for primary targets to accuse directly or implicate indirectly several secondary targets, including both male and female relatives and associates. Discounting all secondary targets would alter the statistical picture significantly. Quaife, however, avoids this result by constructing a double standard, which presupposes, by implication, that early modern Europeans did not 'mean it' when they accused men of being witches but were serious when they accused women. That Quaife is able to suggest this without providing any qualitative evidence of early modern beliefs about male witches indicates the power of statistical figures within witchcraft historiography.[5]

The point here is not to deny that, generally speaking, more women than men were accused of witchcraft. This is a central, indisputable feature of early modern witch-hunting that cannot be ignored. Nevertheless, it is a feature that is far from uniform, and that lack of uniformity must be taken into account in analyses of gender and witchcraft in early modern Europe. The 'big picture' was not monochromatic, even on the often-polarised field of gender; it needs to be shaded in, nuanced, to reflect its polychromatic character. One means of accomplishing this goal is to make the men accused of witchcraft visible through specific case studies.

John Samond, Essex

Our first case study comes from the county of Essex in England. The Calendar of Assize Records contains the well-known Essex indictments, records which Alan Macfarlane plumbed for his path-breaking 1970 study *Witchcraft in Tudor and Stuart England*. Macfarlane noted that Essex witches were usually women, and found that of the twenty-three men accused, 'eleven were either married to an accused witch or appeared in a joint indictment with a woman.'[6] This fact has been reiterated by several authors in order to make the male witches 'invisible', as we argued in our first chapter. Marianne Hester, for instance, barely mentions male witches in her revisionist analysis of the Essex trials, except to remark that '[i]n England more than 90 percent of those formally accused of witchcraft were women, and the few men who were also formally accused tended to be married to an accused witch or to appear jointly with a woman'.[7] Joseph Klaits also refers to the Essex data, using them to support his assertion that 'many of the accused men were implicated solely due to their connection with female suspects.'[8]

These statements, including Macfarlane's, assume that the women involved in the eleven cases were accused first and were the cause of the accusations against the men. This is problematic because the indictments, which provide the bulk of the evidence for any interpretations of witchcraft in Essex, contain little in the way of detailed information about individual cases. In some instances, it is possible to work out who was most likely to have been accused first. For example, in August 1579 Richard Presmary and his wife Joan were indicted and convicted at the Chelmsford Assizes on the charge of murder by witchcraft. Joan Presmary had been indicted for witchcraft in the previous year, at the Brentwood Assizes of July 1578.[9] Richard Presmary had no prior indictments. It seems reasonable that in this case Joan Presmary may have been accused first, because she would have had a reputation as a witch. This tells us nothing about why Richard Presmary would have been accused this time, but it does appear to support the suggestion that men were secondary suspects.

On the other hand, in many cases there is no way of knowing, from the indictments, who was accused first. William and Margery Skelton, a couple from Little Wakering, were indicted and convicted on multiple counts of murder by witchcraft at the Chelmsford Assizes of March 1573. Neither one appears to have had previous indictments. This case is especially interesting because the four murders are divided up evenly between the couple: William bewitched one girl, Margery bewitched another, and the couple committed the remaining murders together. There is nothing in the indictment record to indicate which of the Skeltons first fell under suspicion, or who was the 'lead' witch.[10] Similarly, Richard Dune and Agnes Dunne were indicted for witchcraft together in July 1589; since neither had ever been indicted previously, there is no way of knowing which one of them was the primary suspect.[11]

It may very well have been that in all of these cases it was the woman who first 'attracted' the charge of witchcraft, and that the men were suspected merely because of their association with them. The case of John Samond, however, suggests that it was equally possible for men to be suspected independently; furthermore, this case suggests that women may at times have been the secondary suspects.

John Samond, also known as Smythe, Smith, or Salmon, first appears in the Essex indictment records in July 1560, three years before the Witchcraft Statute of 1563 was passed.[12] On this occasion, he was charged with having bewitched with fatal consequences John Graunte and Bridget Pecocke, who died on 28 May 1560 and 29 August 1560 respectively. He was acquitted the following year, at the Chelmsford Assizes of March 1561.[13] Samond reappears several times in the Essex Assize records, usually on a charge of witchcraft, until his final indictment in 1587, at which point he was found guilty and sentenced to be hanged.[14]

Samond is an important figure because his frequent appearances in the indictment records allow us to compare his charges with those of the women indicted at the same assizes. His indictments demonstrate that, contrary to some of the generalisations described at the beginning of this chapter, men could be accused of witchcraft independently of their female relatives and were not always accused of practising magic that was different from that of women. Indeed, the striking thing about John Samond, besides his frequent appearances before the assizes, is that there is no clear distinction between him and the female witches indicted in Essex.

In 1560, at the time of his first indictment, Samond was a beer-brewer with a reputation. The indictment states that

> John Samond of Danbury..., beer-brewer, otherwise called John Smythe, is a common enchanter and witch as well of men as beasts ... not having God before his eyes, but being moved and seduced by the instigation of the Devil, by the devilish arts of enchantment and witchcraft, on 28 May, 1 Eliz. and diverse days and places as well before as afterwards, at Danbury aforesaid, of his malice aforethought, a certain John (*sic*) Graunte and Brigit Pecocke did

> bewitch and enchant, by reason of which the said Brigit ... until
> 29 August next following did languish, on which day the said
> Brigit ... died. And the said Antony Grant ... from the 28 May in
> the year above said until the 28 May next following did languish,
> on which day the said Antony ... died.[15]

There is no explanation of why or how he bewitched his victims, but
this is normal for indictments, which are very terse documents. What is
interesting here is the identification of Samond as a 'common enchanter
and witch'.[16] The language used to describe him is the same as that used
to describe a woman, Margery Stanton, at the 1579 Chelmsford Lent
sessions. In Latin, the indictment against Samond reads: 'Johanes
Samond ... communis incantator ac fascinator tam hominum quam ani-
malium'.[17] The indictment against Stanton is virtually identical:
'Margeria Stanton ... existens communis incantatrix et fascinatrix tam
hominum quam bestiarum et aliarum rerum'.[18] The two witches are dif-
ferentiated only by the use of appropriate masculine and feminine end-
ings for the words 'incantator/ incantatrix' and 'fascinator/fascinatrix'.
If English people believed that there was an essential distinction
between male and female witches (as witches), this is not reflected in
their legal language.[19]

Samond's next appearance at the assizes, in March 1570, was on a
charge of grand larceny. He was accused of stealing sheep from two
other men, found guilty, but allowed benefit of clergy.[20] At the same
assizes, two women, both from the village of Little Baddow, were
indicted for murder by witchcraft; one was found guilty, the other
acquitted.[21]

In August 1572, John Samond was indicted again for witchcraft.
This time, he is listed as a yeoman and beer-brewer, and his wife Joan is
indicted with him. This case is important for what it suggests – or, more
precisely, for what it does not suggest – regarding the relationship
between male witches and their wives.

We have seen that modern scholars tend to assume a causal relationship in which the man is accused because of his association with a

female witch. Although there is not enough information given in the indictments to say with any certainty what the background to this case was, it seems unlikely that suspicion of Joan Samond would have led to suspicion against her husband, instead of the other way around. John Samond had a reputation for witchcraft that had landed him in court before, whereas this was his wife's first indictment. Furthermore, the charges themselves suggest that suspicion may have fallen on John first. The first charge against John Samond is for bewitching to death two cows belonging to William Treasure. This is the most recent of the three bewitchings listed in the indictment and, significantly, Treasure had given evidence against Samond in the 1570 sheep-stealing case. Treasure may have suspected an act of revenge and accused John Samond; the other charges against John and his wife (maiming one man and laming another) may have been brought forward subsequently.[22]

Two other witchcraft cases at this session show that the type of charges against John Samond were not gender-specific. Agnes Francys was found guilty of bewitching a horse and three people, and Agnes Steademan was found guilty of bewitching a woman and four cows so that they became 'violently ill'.[23] In 1587, Samond was indicted for murdering a woman by witchcraft. Three women, indicted at the same assizes, were charged with killing livestock and a person by witchcraft.[24] There is nothing in these indictments to suggest that there was a divide between men's and women's witchcraft.

The main difference between Samond and the women accused of witchcraft at the same assizes is that the women (except for his own wife) were generally found guilty, while he was acquitted. It is tempting to conclude that Samond was acquitted because he was a man; however, it is important to remember that conviction rates for witchcraft in England were relatively low for both women and men. On the Home Circuit, fewer than half of the witchcraft indictments resulted in convictions, and only 22 per cent of those indicted were executed.[25] In English witchcraft trials, a guilty verdict was by no means a foregone conclusion, and there are many cases in the Essex records of women going free.

In any case, Samond's luck ran out later in 1587, at an assize session that demonstrates how difficult it is to draw solid conclusions about the role of gender in witchcraft prosecutions. Samond was indicted at the Chelmsford Assizes in July, on the charges of bewitching Henry Hove 'so that he languished until 5 Apr. and then died' and of killing a cow by witchcraft. Samond was tried before a grand jury, found guilty, and sentenced to be hanged. At the same session, two women were also indicted for witchcraft: they were acquitted.[26]

Despite Samond's many indictments, we do not know very much about him. There is simply not enough information in the indictments to enable us to say with any certainty why he was finally convicted in 1587. If all of the accused witches at that assize session had been convicted, we could surmise that they faced a 'hanging' jury that simply found everyone guilty; but the acquittal of the two women prevents us from reaching that conclusion. Perhaps, after twenty-seven years, Samond had exhausted the court's and community's patience. We cannot know, and in that sense John Samond does not help us establish explanatory models; but then, that is why he is so valuable. Samond is almost as much of a nuisance to modern scholars looking for patterns as he was to his community of Danbury. He muddles the patterns, and in doing so forces us to re-examine our assumptions about both male and female witches.

Chonrad Stoeckhlin, Oberstdorf

From 1587 to 1592, a wave of witch trials rolled across the prince-bishopric of Augsburg. In one district, Oberdorf, the trials claimed sixty-eight lives: 'the single largest persecution to be found anywhere between the Danube River and the Alps.'[27] This wave began in the judicial district of Rettenberg in 1586, when Chonrad Stoeckhlin, a herdsman in the alpine village of Oberstdorf, accused Anna Enzensbergerin of being a witch. Stoeckhlin's accusation initiated a series of trials that resulted in the executions of approximately twenty-five people, including Stoeckhlin himself. Although both men and women were accused during the course of the trials, all of those executed in the district of Rettenberg, except for Stoeckhlin, were women.[28]

This case appears, on the surface, to reflect a simple anti-female dynamic. Several women were burned at the stake on the word of a man, and those men who were also accused managed to escape the fire. Wolfgang Behringer, whose microhistory of Chonrad Stoeckhlin provides the basis for this discussion, suggests, plausibly, that the court accepted accusations against women more readily than accusations against men, and that men were more likely to flee when they were accused.[29] The fact that one man was executed may not seem significant when viewed against the number of women who died.

The case of Chonrad Stoeckhlin *is* significant, however, precisely because the trials at Rettenberg were so biased against women. In a context that appears almost uniformly misogynist, Stoeckhlin, like John Samond, confuses the pattern and forces us to ask more questions about the relationship of gender to witch trials and contemporary knowledge about witches. Also like Samond, Stoeckhlin fails on several counts to fit the model of the male witch constructed by modern scholars. He was accused independently of a close female relative (there was a connection with a female relative, but not in a way which conforms to the model: see note 43); he was accused at the very beginning of a witch panic, not in its later stages; and he was accused of the most stereotypical elements of witchcraft: the pact with the Devil, night flight to the Sabbath, and sexual intercourse with the Devil.

How did Stoeckhlin become a witch? His complex path to the stake has been reconstructed by Wolfgang Behringer from the court records of his trial. Born in 1549, Chonrad Stoeckhlin was the horse wrangler of Oberstdorf, a position of responsibility and considerable status. According to Behringer, 'The post of horse wrangler was the most eminent in the hierarchy of herdsmen, well above the more numerous herdsmen for oxen, cows, goats, sheep, and geese. ... [H]orses were regarded as prestige animals, whose care demanded the greatest attention and the highest qualifications.' Stoeckhlin was married, and he and his wife had seven children, of whom only two survived infancy. He inherited his position as horse wrangler when his father went blind in 1567. His mother died in 1571, a year of famine. Stoeckhlin and his family were not wealthy, but they seem to have been comfortable: they had a house and were able to keep a cow in the wintertime.[30]

In February 1578, Stoeckhlin and his friend Jacob Walch, an oxherd, spent an evening drinking wine and talking about death and the afterlife. They made a pact with each other that 'whichever of the two should die first should come to the other one ... and [should] show him what it is like in that world.' Eight days later, Walch died suddenly. After another eight days, while Stoeckhlin was out in the woods, Walch's spirit appeared to him and told him to repent his sins.[31] Stoeckhlin and his family took this instruction seriously, and after a year of penance Stoeckhlin was rewarded by a visit from what would turn out to be his personal angel. This angel, which Stoeckhlin described to his interrogators as 'a person dressed in white with a red cross on his (or her) forehead', transported him to 'a strange and distant place' where he witnessed 'pain and joy'. The angel became Stoeckhlin's 'soul-guide'; it appeared several times a year to take him on soul-journeys as part of a group Stoeckhlin called the phantoms of the night (*die Nachtschar*).[32]

In addition to his responsibilities as a herdsman, Stoeckhlin was a healer.[33] It was not unusual for herdsmen to function as healers of both animals and humans: 'Herdsmen served ... as veterinarians; like blacksmiths, midwives, and executioners, their help was much in demand for human sicknesses too', including illnesses caused by magic.[34] Stoeckhlin's contact with the supernatural realm of the *Nachtschar* increased his perceived powers and led his fellow villagers to connect his healing abilities to special powers of identifying those who had caused magical illnesses. He became a witch-finder: he named the witches responsible for injuries and sicknesses, and knew how to force them, ritually, to undo their evil magic.[35]

In the spring of 1586, someone in Oberstdorf consulted Stoeckhlin about a string of injuries. The horse wrangler determined that a sixty-year-old woman, Anna Enzensbergerin, was the culprit, and urged her to reverse her spell. Instead of doing so, however, Enzensbergerin fled the village for a time. When she returned, the authorities of Oberstdorf arrested her on 'the bare testimony' of Stoeckhlin, who had learned she was a witch from the leader of the night phantoms. This accusation would prove to be Stoeckhlin's undoing. The district authorities sent an inquiry regarding the case to the Dillingen Ruling Council. The Council ruled that Enzensbergerin should be held in custody, Chonrad Stoeckhlin should be questioned, and an executioner should be found 'who would know "how to torture these kinds of people"'. Around 27 July, Stoeckhlin was arrested and taken to Fluhenstein Castle, near Sonthofen. His first hearing took place on 29 July, when he was questioned by the district judge, district governor, and county clerk.[36]

Why arrest Stoeckhlin, a respectable and respected member of the community, whose powers were for healing, not harming, people? Stoeckhlin was not, by our standards, and certainly not by his own, a witch; however, the officials of the bishopric of Augsburg seem to have found it all too easy to suspect him of being one. They knew that he had accused Enzensbergerin, and they knew about his nocturnal flights. At the first hearing, they questioned Stoeckhlin about his journeys. He explained that there were three kinds of journey: that of the *Nachtschar*; the 'righteous journey' in which 'the dead are led to their places'; and the witches' flight. Stoeckhlin said that he never flew with the witches and knew nothing about their flight, but his story meshed too well with his learned interrogators' knowledge of witches to allay their suspicions. Aerial flight, at night, with a group of mysterious men and women, led by an 'angel'… as far as the authorities were concerned, what Stoeckhlin described to them was the witches' flight to the Sabbath, led by Stoeckhlin's 'sex-devil'.[37] Their image of Stoeckhlin was not improved when Anna Enzensbergerin and Barbara Luzin, his deceased mother's stepsister, not only confessed to being witches but also claimed that they had learned all they knew from Stoeckhlin's mother, Ursula Schedlerin. Ironically, Stoeckhlin had accused both women himself.[38]

[55]

necessarily female. This perspective assumes, in effect, that the men who suspected and condemned Chonrad Stoeckhlin made a category error; not conforming to their own intellectual system. This … be implicit in most work on male witches, … no reason to believe, that … resonance when …

… sans.
… arts of
… n the two
… s, both male

… ew Romney, Kent,
… ours accused him of
… ng horses, and killing a
… n and a daughter, were not
… him was thrown out.[50] That
… bout their accusations may be
… act a confession' after Godfrey joked
… iam Clarke attacked Godfrey with
… e.[51]

… inted out that Godfrey, a middling house-
… r and landlord, and active participant in civic
… stereotype of the 'elderly, marginal widow depend-
… e equally socially-ambivalent younger single woman
… the conventional expectations of her neighbours, often
… as a classic tale of fear and *maleficium*.' The case raises the
… he way historians classify aspects of the past': as Gaskill says, 'we
… her explain away the social identity of the accused as an exception
… rule or, more fruitfully, we can redefine the rule to accommodate that
… dentity within a broader interpretative scheme.'[52]

Richard Kieckhefer has probed the beginnings on the 'elaborated
concept' during the 1430s in the western Swiss canton of Vaud. A
slightly later manuscript (Archives Cantonales Vaudoises, Ac 29) shows
that of the nineteen people it lists as having been tried for witchcraft

[58]

On the basis of Stoeckhlin's initial hearing and the confessions of Enzensbergerin and Luzin, the district officials compiled a lengthy questionnaire of 146 items. The questions reveal the primary elements of their belief that Stoeckhlin was a witch: no one could recognise witches unless he already belonged to their society; the *Nachtschar* were really witches flying to the Sabbath; Stoeckhlin's angel was a black sex-devil; Stoeckhlin's mother was a witch; and several of Stoeckhlin's children had died early, possibly sacrificed to the Devil or used to make witches' salves.[39] They interrogated Stoeckhlin again in November and December, gradually forcing his original narrative to conform to theirs. Stoeckhlin was tortured brutally, and confessed in December to all of the charges in the questionnaire. His ordeal came to an end on 23 January 1587, when he was burned at the stake. He spent over six months in prison, was subjected to tortures which nearly killed him, and was transformed by the official process from a healer and witch-finder into a witch.[40]

There is nothing about Stoeckhlin's case to set him apart from the thousands of other witches who were accused, tried and condemn[ed] early modern Europe. By the time his interrogators were finis[hed] Stoeckhlin had become, from a learned point of view, the most ste[reo] typical witch imaginable. He flew on a goat; he attended the Sabba[th] where he and the other witches 'danced, feasted, and copulated'; he ha[d] a demon lover; he renounced God and made a pact with the Devil;[41] h[e] murdered his own children; he practised harmful magic; he had a Devil'[s] mark; and he could transform himself into an animal.[42] The only thing 'wrong' with the picture is that Stoeckhlin was not an old, poor, marginal woman, but a fairly young man with a family and a decent living.

If we look at Chonrad Stoeckhlin from a perspective coloured by conventional assumptions about male witches, we might be tempted to dismiss him as an aberration who adds nothing to our understanding of witchcraft and gender. A male witch who was accused at the beginning of a witch-hunt, independently of a female relative,[43] and charged with every diabolic element in the early modern learned concept of witchcraft, looks very strange if one is committed to the idea that 'real' witches are

with the Devil, attending the witches' Sabbath, owning books of magic, and causing the demonic possessions of several Ursuline nuns. Evidence against Grandier included the presence of several Devil's marks on his body. It was very common for witches to be searched f[or] Devil's marks, and for them to be found on or near the most secret p[...] These insensitive spots were found 'in the two buttocks close to his anus, and [...] [Grandier's] body, in the two buttocks close to his anus, and [...] testicles'.[48] After Grandier's arrest, many of his associate[s...] and female, were accused of being witches.[49]

Finally, William Godfrey, a yeoman farmer in N[...] was charged with witchcraft in 1617. His neigh[bours...] various *maleficia*, including laming lambs, kill[ing...] child. Godfrey's wife and two children, a so[n...] accused of witchcraft, and the case agains[t...] Godfrey's neighbours were serious [...] inferred from an assault on him. W[...] a cudgel 'in a vain attempt to ex[...] about bewitching Clarke's ma[...]

Malcolm Gaskill has [...] holder, prosperous farm[...] life, does not match the [...] ent on charity, or t[...] who fails to mee[t...] her female pe[...] also be rea[d...] issue of [...] can e[...] to [...]

typical witch who [...] He even 'suckle[d] the apparti[...] so many female witches were supposed to hav[e...] In a more spectacular case, the Jesuit priest Urbain [...] executed in 1634 at Loudun, having been found guilty of making a pac[t...]

between 1438 and 1498, twelve were men. In the trials of Pierre Munier (1448) and François Marguet of Dommartin (1498), the men were accused of precisely the same kind of crimes as women were: renouncing God, doing homage to the Devil, attending 'sects' or 'synagogues' of witches, eating the flesh of infants, and misdeeds such as profanation of the Eucharist or killing persons or animals.[53]

Such an interpretative scheme needs to take into account the similarities between male and female witches. As the examples presented in this chapter demonstrate, the social identities of witches were variable, but, once labelled as such, they all fit within the framework of early modern beliefs about witches as Devil-worshippers and practitioners of *maleficium*. This does not mean that there were no differences between male and female witches. Lyndal Roper has found that in sixteenth-century Augsburg there was 'a gendered specialization in the practice of sorcery itself', which 'emerges most vividly in the different ways male and female sorcerers made use of parts of the body in sorcery.' Men used written spells and 'more exotic bodily relics derived from criminals' (see figure 1), while women used more spoken spells and 'the natural magical properties of the body.'[54] Eva Labouvie and Willem de Blécourt have also found differences in the types of witchcraft attributed to men and women.[55] These findings are important and certainly worthy of further investigation; however, these fine distinctions should not obscure the fact that conventional modern generalisations about male witches have created a false dichotomy between the men and women accused of witchcraft and have imposed on the past a narrow conception of early modern attitudes toward gender and witchcraft. Gaskill's closing comments about William Godfrey and his accusers are appropriate: 'Godfrey's case may well have been atypical, but to the people of New Romney in 1617 – not least Godfrey himself – it was as valid and real an experience of the European "witch-craze" as any other prosecution in the early modern period.'[56]

In order to be meaningful, our interpretative frameworks have to be just as capable of accommodating the atypical experiences as they are of

1 Male and female witches exhuming a dead body (foreground), cutting up a dead baby (middle) and cutting down a hanged felon (background), all for the use of body parts and instruments used for executions to make noxious charms, potions and ointments.

accommodating the typical. In the case of early modern ideas about witches, this means adopting a flexible approach to issues of gender that recognises the commonalities between male and female witches and the validity of early modern ideas and experiences.

Notes

1 Briggs, *Witches and Neighbors*, 263.
2 Sources for table 1: Monter, *Witchcraft in France and Switzerland*, 119, table 7; Gabor Klaniczay, 'Hungary: The accusations and the universe of popular magic', *Centres and Peripheries*, 219–255: 222, table 8.1; *Calendar of Assize Records: Essex Indictments: Elizabeth I*, ed. J.S. Cockburn (London: HMSO, 1978); Midelfort, *Witch Hunting in*

Southwestern Germany, 181, table 14, Karlsen, *The Devil in the Shape of a Woman*, 48–49, tables 1 and 2; Larner, *Enemies of God*, 91; Hans Eyvind Naess, 'Norway: The criminological context', *Centres and Peripheries*, 367–382: 371, table 14.1, and 378; Midelfort, *Witch Hunting in Southwestern Germany*, 181, table 14; Ruth Martin, *Witchcraft and the Inquisition in Venice 1550–1650* (Oxford: Basil Blackwell, 1989), 226; Per Sörlin, *'Wicked Arts': Witchcraft and Magic Trials in Southern Sweden, 1635–1754* (Leiden: Brill, 1999), 122, table 5.4; Monter, *Witchcraft in France and Switzerland*, 119, table 7; Marijke Gijswijt-Hofstra, 'Witchcraft before Zeeland magistrates and church councils, sixteenth to twentieth centuries', *Witchcraft in the Netherlands from the Fourteenth to the Twentieth Century*, eds. Marijke Gijswijt-Hofstra and Willem Frijhoff, trans. Rachel M.J. van der Wilden-Fall (Rotterdam: Rotterdam University Press, 1991 [1987]), 103–111: 110–111; Monter, *Witchcraft in France and Switzerland*, 119, table 7; Antero Heikkinen and Timo Kervinen, 'Finland: The male domination', *Centres and Peripheries*, 319–338: 321; Monter, 'Toads and eucharists', 564 n. 1. Data from the Parlement of Burgundy; Maia Madar, 'Estonia I: Werewolves and poisoners', *Centres and Peripheries*, 257–272: 267, table 9.2; Monter, 'Toads and eucharists', 584, table 3; Kirsten Hastrup, 'Iceland: Sorcerers and paganism', *Centres and Peripheries*, 383–401: 386.

3 Joseph Klaits, *Servants of Satan: The Age of the Witch Hunts* (Bloomington: Indiana University Press, 1985), 51.

4 G.R. Quaife, 'Gender, sex and misogyny: I', *Godly Zeal and Furious Rage: The Witch in Early Modern Europe* (New York: St Martin's, 1987), 79–96: 81.

5 Willem de Blécourt has argued that '[c]ounting women is misleading precisely because they were accused of behaving as non-women, of failing to adhere to the social norm of femininity.' 'The making of the female witch', 293.

6 Macfarlane, *Witchcraft in Tudor and Stuart England*, 160. Our count of male witches in the Essex records is 24, not 23.

7 Marianne Hester, *Lewd Women and Wicked Witches: A Study in the Dynamics of Male Domination* (London and New York: Routledge, 1992), 108.

8 Klaits, *Servants of Satan*, 52.

9 *Essex Indictments*, record nos. 1084 (Richard and Joan Presmary) and 1010 (Joan Presmary). The indictment for the joint case states that on 10 January 1579 the couple bewitched a bricklayer, Gabriel Smythe, so that he died on 17 July 1579. There is no obvious connection with Joan Presmary's individual case.

10 *Ibid.*, record no. 620. The deaths attributed to the Skeltons dated back to 1568.

11 *Ibid.*, record no. 2000. The Dun(n)es were charged with bewitching a gelding and two men. They were found not guilty. The record does not actually state that Agnes was Richard's wife.

12 On the Witchcraft Statute of 1563, see James Sharpe, 'The theological and legal bases for witch-hunting', *Instruments of Darkness: Witchcraft in England 1550–1750* (London: Penguin, 1997 [n.p.: Hamish Hamilton, 1996]), 80–102: 90.

13 *Essex Indictments*, record nos. 95 and 109. In record no. 95, Cockburn gives the dates of death as 29 August for Graunte and 29 May for Pecocke; in record no. 109, the dates are 29 August for Graunte and 28 May for Pecocke. We have accepted the death dates given in C.L'Estrange Ewen, *Witch Hunting and Witch Trials: The Indictments for Witchcraft from the Records of 1373 Assizes held for the Home Circuit A.D. 1559–1736* (New York: Dial, 1929), 77–78. Transcription and translation of the Chelmsford 1560 indictment, which corresponds to *Essex Indictments* no 95.

14 *Ibid.*, complete references to John Samond, alias Smythe, Salmon, Smith: record nos. 95, 108–110, 418, 423, 561, 568, 571, 1699–1700, 1704, 1729, 1790, 1792.

15 Ewen, *Witch Hunting and Witch Trials*, 78. Transcription and translation of the full indictment against Samond, which is listed by Ewen as indictment no. 1.

16 *Essex Indictments*, record no. 95. Samond was indicted originally in Queen's Bench, but his case was transferred to assizes 30 Jan. 1561. He was tried by jury in March 1561 and found not guilty. Record nos. 108–110.

17 Ewen, *Witch Hunting and Witch Trials*, 77.

18 *Ibid.*, 81. Indictment no. 122 (record no.1063 in *Essex Indictments*).

19 In *Essex Indictments*, Cockburn translates 'communis incantator ac fascinator' as 'common wizard'. See our Introduction for comments on the use of 'wizard'.

20 *Essex Indictments*, record no. 423.

21 *Ibid.*, record nos. 428 (Alice Swallow) and 429 (Alice Bainbricke).

22 *Ibid.*, record no. 571 (Ewen no. 56). Cockburn's version of the indictment is a synthesis of several separate indictments. Ewen's transcription of the charge of harming Edward Robynson is very interesting: the indictment is in Latin, but uses the English words 'witchcraftes inchantementes charmes & sorceries'. Ewen, *Witch Hunting and Witch Trials*, 79–80.

23 Essex Indictments, record nos, 580 (Francys) and 582 (Steademan).

24 *Ibid.*, record nos. 1704 (Samond), 1730 (Joan and Frances Preston), and 1731 (Rose Clarens).

25 Sharpe, *Instruments of Darkness*, 111.

26 *Essex Indictments*, record nos. 1792 (Samond), 1795 (Joan Gibson), and 1793 (Alice Bust).

27 Wolfgang Behringer, *Shaman of Oberstdorf: Chonrad Stoeckhlin and the Phantoms of the Night*, trans. H.C. Erik Midelfort (Charlottesville, VA: Virginia University Press, 1998; orig. *Chonrad Stoeckhlin und die Nachtschar: eine Geschichte aus der frühen Neuzeit*, Munich, 1994), 116.

28 *Ibid.*, 114. For a summary of the events which places them within a wider German context, see Wolfgang Behringer, *Witchcraft Persecutions in Bavaria: Popular Magic, Religious Zealotry and Reason of State in Early Modern Europe*, trans. J.C. Grayson and David Lederer (Cambridge: Cambridge University Press, 1997; orig. *Hexenverfolgung in Bayern: Volksmagie, Glaubenseifer und Straaträson in der Frühen Neuzeit*, Munich: 1987), 115–211, esp. 124–5, 177–180.

29 Behringer, *Shaman of Oberstdorf*, 114.

30 *Ibid.*, 4–6.

31 *Ibid.*, 11–13.

32 *Ibid.*, 17–23. See Behringer for a full discussion of *die Nachtschar* and parallels with similar folklore, e.g. the *benandanti* described by Carlo Ginzburg.

33 *Ibid.*, 83.

34 *Ibid.*, 7.

35 *Ibid.*, 84.

36 *Ibid.*, 90–92.

37 *Ibid.*, 92–95.

38 *Ibid.*, 99–100.

39 *Ibid.*, 95.

40 *Ibid.*, 102–105.

41 *Ibid.*, 103–104.

42 *Ibid.*, 100.

43 Behringer places great emphasis on the charge that Stoeckhlin's mother was a witch, stating at one point that 'Stoeckhlin's participation in the society of witches was obviously deduced from the notion that being a witch was inheritable' (*ibid.*, 105). Elsewhere, he suggests that 'being related to a witch was enough to prompt the suspicion that one was a witch' (118). This emphasis seems greatly overstated. According to the chronology of the case, Stoeckhlin was already under suspicion, on totally independent grounds, before anyone mentioned that his mother had been a witch.

Furthermore, if the inheritability of witchness was so essential, why were Stoeckhlin's wife and children never called for questioning (118)?

44 Jonathan Pearl, 'Witchcraft in New France in the seventeenth century: The social aspect', *Historical Reflections/Réflexions Historiques* 4, no. 1 (1977): 191–205: 193.

45 Karlsen, *The Devil in the Shape of a Woman*, 49.

46 'George Burroughs', *Salem-Village Witchcraft: A Documentary Record of Local Conflict in Colonial New England*, eds. Paul Boyer and Stephen Nissenbaum (Boston: Northeastern University Press, 1993 [1972]), 67–90. Burroughs was said, for instance, to possess extraordinary strength.

47 'Testimony of Susanna Sheldon', *Salem-Village Witchcraft*, 55–57: 56. Sheldon also testified that Elizabeth Colson 'suckled, as it appeared, a yellow bird'.

48 Robert Rapley, *A Case of Witchcraft: The Trial of Urbain Grandier* (Montreal and Kingston: McGill-Queen's University Press, 1998), 151. Anne Barstow has emphasised the sexual nature of searching for marks on *women's* bodies; it can hardly have been less sexual, or less invasive, to search for marks in the private parts of men's bodies.

49 *Ibid.*, 159–162.

50 Gaskill, 'The Devil in the shape of a man', 151–156. Willem de Blécourt has remarked of this case that '[t]he accusations of bewitchments against William Godfrey … can be interpreted within the parameters of Godfrey's reputation as a thief of sheep.' 'The making of the female witch', 308 n. 63.

51 Gaskill, 'The Devil in the shape of a man', 157.

52 *Ibid.*, 158–159.

53 Lecture of 18 March 2002, in the Department of History and Classics, University of Alberta.

54 Roper, 'Exorcism and the theology of the body', *Oedipus and the Devil*, 171–198: 188–190.

55 de Blécourt, 'The making of the female witch'; Labouvie, 'Männer im Hexenprozess'.

56 Gaskill, 'The Devil in the shape of a man', 170.

3

TORTURED CONFESSIONS: AGENCY AND SELFHOOD AT STAKE

One of the central issues of current research, especially of feminist research into early modern witchcraft, is the question of (female) agency. The stereotype of female passivity in the face of male oppression has been contested, and we have now a far more sophisticated understanding of women and their varied means of expressing agency and resistance than was possible in a system of reference based on victimhood. Witchcraft trials, perhaps paradoxically, have proven to be fruitful sites for finding evidence of women's resistance and agency. Women accused of witchcraft resisted in various ways, including the recantation of confessions made under torture. This very resistance, particularly recantation, has led to some highly questionable interpretations of witchcraft cases. On one hand, it is necessary to recognise the possibility of resistance and the role of the accused witch in shaping the narrative of his or her confession. To speak as if confession under torture were simply inevitable erases the struggles of accused witches.[1] On the other hand, it is possible to take the recognition of agency too far, and to distort experiences and motivations. Women and men were influenced by the operations of power, but also influenced these in turn. Agency theory posits that actors always have choices, no matter how restricted; 'agent-centred' morality proposes a novel twist on both traditional Kantian internalist categories and a useful political starting point for taking agents' conscious moral choices seriously.[2]

In this chapter, we address the problems of both male and female witches' agency and selfhood. Issues of agency and resistance are not specific to women, even if women have been foregrounded in studies relating to both concepts. We have seen that it was quite possible that a majority, even a large majority, of accused witches in a given region might be men. Ideas about male witches and accusations against them may have differed somewhat from those concerning women, but in general they were more alike than unlike. Therefore, we must apply questions regarding agency and resistance to cases involving men as well as to those involving women.

We approach agency and resistance first through a critique of Lyndal Roper's psychoanalytical reading of witchcraft confessions, then through an analysis of witchcraft trials that involved what Wolfgang Behringer has dubbed 'the elaborated concept of witchcraft', the theory of satanic allegiance typically invoked during 'epidemic' episodes of witch-hunting, thereby bracketing out most accusations involving 'minor' witchcraft, popular magic, healing spells, potions and the like.[3]

The scholar of early modern witchcraft faces a number of difficult methodological and epistemological problems, most of which stem from the 'impossible' nature of witchcraft itself. The problem of how to read and assess 'non-factual' witchcraft materials – that is, witchcraft trial testimony – is central to witchcraft scholarship.[4] However, the troubled relationship between witchcraft scholars and their materials goes deeper. Research into early modern witch-hunting and ideas about witches is closely dependent on witchcraft trials; indeed, without the trials, there could be very little of such research at all. Even the intellectual historian of witchcraft, putatively uninterested in actual prosecutions, works with materials that are linked closely with trials: the authors of late medieval and early modern demonological treatises drew heavily on trial accounts for evidence to develop and sustain their arguments. These treatises, in turn, contributed to the evolution of learned witchcraft theory and thus to the dynamics and patterns of witchcraft prosecutions.

On one level, this is merely stating the obvious. But, when one considers more carefully the central role of trials in the production of witchcraft materials, it becomes apparent that modern scholars are locked into an intimate relationship with processes that involved the deliberate infliction of extreme suffering. We may decry the methods of interrogators and torturers, or express admiration and sympathy for accused witches, but we remain in the uncomfortable position of benefiting – intellectually and professionally – from the ordeals of others. This is not to suggest that we should stop studying witchcraft, any more than we should stop studying the history of warfare, science, or any other subject. Our research, however, needs to be accompanied by serious reflection on the ethics of representing others. Such reflection, we submit, is lacking in witchcraft studies, with scholars preserving virtual silence on the ethical, as opposed to methodological or political, problems associated with writing about witches and witchcraft. It is important to state that we are not opposed to multiple readings of historical materials, nor to postmodern approaches. We are, however, opposed to readings – of any school – that treat human subjects as blank slates upon which a historian may inscribe whatever he or she wishes. Historians have great freedom in their interpretations simply because their subjects are dead. This ought to be regarded as a privilege, not as a right. It is unethical to use that freedom to shape our representation of historical subjects to serve us and our (political) agendas without any thought of serving them, preserving their memory, and *re*-presenting them.[5]

To the extent that we have access – via distorting, rhetorically charged tropes and textualisations, to be sure – to historical actors' categories, we are bound to take them seriously as historical factors, no matter how silly, naive or misguided they might seem to, say, a pragmatic suburban car salesman or a worldly advertising executive. It is quite true, as Lyndal Roper has suggested, that we cannot read witchcraft confessions as straightforward documents susceptible to analysis by traditional methods such as 'historical realism'.[6] However, we are licensed to examine the documents for traces not merely of the interrogators' knowledge or theory that shaped the proceedings, but also for the resistances and principles that shaped the contributions of the accused witch. Roper intended to do this, but was blocked from doing so with an open mind by the ideological engagements she brought to her sources.

In her much-reviewed and highly original collection *Oedipus and the Devil: Witchcraft, Sexuality and Religion in Early Modern Europe*, Roper approached the topic of witchcraft confessions and their recantation from a psychoanalytic perspective. One of Roper's great accomplishments in this book, composed of nine substantial and thematically related articles or chapters, was to call into question traditional feminist approaches to domestic and sexual power politics as expressed in her first book, *The Holy Household: Women and Morals in Reformation Augsburg*.[7] Arguing in *Oedipus and the Devil* that women who endure sexual oppression and even abuse in patriarchal societies are more than just victims, Roper applied assiduously and to impressive effect the by-now familiar theory of limited agency: not only the powerful, but also the oppressed have and make choices and respond even to abuse in ways that make it easier for them to live with misery and with themselves; suppressed rebellion is still rebellion and evidence of it discredits misogynistic narratives of passivity.[8] This theory turns out to be both useful to us, because it helps us to understand the actions of some accused witches, and useful to Roper's psychoanalytic agenda, as it gives her a political structure into which to fit otherwise strange, even self-incriminating statements and actions.

Roper was interested in the motivations for confession and theoretical explanations designed to get behind them. Regina Bartholome (Augsburg, 1670) provided a case study that gave the original paper and the entire collection its name.[9] Regina, aged twenty-one when she was tried for witchcraft, confessed that she was a witch. Roper argued that 'the fantasy of witch-hood is created in a project of collaboration between questioner and accused, and that the dynamic by which it progressed can indeed be usefully explained psychoanalytically.'[10] In Regina's case, Roper suggested, Oedipal tensions and self-destructive tendencies combined to produce a dramatic confession to witchcraft and Devil-worship.

In another essay in the same collection ('Witchcraft and fantasy'), Roper uses the case of Anna Ebeler, a lying-in maid who was executed as a witch at Augsburg in 1669, to elaborate on her understanding of witchcraft confessions as products of collusion between the witch and her interrogators. This collusion was not entered into freely by the accused witch, but was a last hope of steering and participating in the elaboration of a confession.[11] This would be a very subtle and deep-reaching insight into the process by which witchcraft accusations and confessions were concocted, but for Roper's sense that more was at play than simple collusion as a result of exercising a restricted but crucial agency. While she dutifully invoked the limitations and qualifications clearly attendant upon any application of Freudian theory to pre-modern individuals, psychosexual complexions and complexes, Roper eventually let go of all pretence and put accused witches from Bavaria and Swabia on a Viennese couch. Roper argued – and this is strong stuff – that in the 'play' (her word) of torture, confession, retraction, re-torture, re-confession and further recantation, the witch participated in sexually charged ways in her own destruction.

Despite this profoundly partisan reading of women's motivations, one of the great accomplishments of Roper's book was to reconnect female physicality with women's experience of life (in the early modern world) as regards maternity, sex, nurturing infants and children, and most especially, gender relations. In the context of witch-hunting and interrogation, Roper argued that we must take female physicality and reproductive differences from men seriously. Female witches were often accused of 'bad nurture', of making suckling infants or children wither, shrivel up, fail to thrive, and die. The recognition that many women accused of witchcraft (at least at Augsburg) were lying-in maids charged by the mothers of babies who got sick or failed to thrive has helped to build a more nuanced historiography relating to witch-hunting.[12] Female physicality had other implications. Roper speculated that in consequence of the forced intimacy between torturer and witch, always figured as a woman, an intimate relationship developed. It was built on the physical incursions of the torturer on the woman's flesh and his services afterwards in binding up the wounds. Thus, 'a bond of intense personal dependence on the part of the witch on her persecutor [*sic*] might be established.'[13] The conditional mood of the auxiliary verb 'might' is crucial; and it would be much harder to make the same argument and to adduce the same psychosexual consequences if the witch were a man. The notion of sexually charged collusion between executioner and witch relies very largely on the preconception that witches were women. Indeed, Roper discussed no male witches at all.

Roper explicitly sexualised the process of torture using banal language from the well-worn repertoire of Freudian sexology:

> Once the torturer's application of pain had brought the witch to confess, she knew she faced execution, and she knew her executioner. In the procedure of interrogation itself, carried out in the presence of council interrogators, scribes and executioner, there is an unmistakable *sado-masochistic* logic, as the witch, in response to pain, might reveal details of her crimes only to deny them subsequently; or as she proffered scattered scraps of information about diabolic sex only then to *tantalize* her questioners with contradiction or silence. In this *sadistic game* of showing and concealing, the witch *forced* her persecutors to apply and reapply pain, prising her body apart to find her secret. Once it was found, she might herself *identify with* the aggressor [italics added throughout].[14]

To suggest that a witch, no matter how much she 'directed' her confessions and recantations, was engaged in a *sado-masochistic* undertaking, or that she *tantalised* her tormentor, or even *forced* him to apply pain, is both to distort the concept of agency and to subordinate agency to unconscious drives. This distorts the accused witch's role in the interrogation dynamic in the service of psychoanalytic theory. Roper's language is laden with implications that the accused witch derived benefit or pleasure from the experience of interrogation under torture, or that she was, on some level, a willing participant. It is, of course, within the realm of possibility, however unlikely, that an individual witch might respond to interrogation in this way. Roy Porter has alluded to the sado-masochistic sexual tendencies in Romantic literary depictions of witches and witch trials; one wonders about the lenses through which modern scholars view the topic, and where these lenses originate.[15]

Evidence from other early modern witchcraft cases, as well as accounts by modern torture survivors, suggests that Roper has paid insufficient attention to the complex relationship between the devastating effects of torture and the struggle of the torture victim to maintain a sense of identity. The fact that an accused witch prolonged her ordeal by recanting does not necessarily mean that she was engaged in a pathological, self-destructive game. Occam's razor allows – perhaps requires – us to posit much simpler explanations for such behaviour: confession was offered to stop torture, but recantations were made for totally different reasons, and not to elicit more torture or as part of a sado-masochistic engagement. To believe as Roper seems to do is to bind the statements and explicit self-justifications of those accused of witchcraft to a procrustean bed.

An example from eighteenth-century Zug in the Swiss Confederacy shows that witches could be tortured into confessing, then recant repeatedly without any evidence of Oedipal or other Freudian complexes at work. In the trials at Zug in 1737, Marx Stadlin and his daughter Euphemia withstood all the horrific tortures applied to them and refused to confess to anything, and were therefore released. However, Anna Maria Stadlin, Marx's wife, said 'she would rather say that she was a witch than be tortured so – she was already half dead'. Nevertheless, in keeping with her husband's and daughter's strong faith, she recanted six times, until she collapsed finally under repeated torture and confessed one last time.[16] Her motivation to confess and recant repeatedly might have had something to do with the kind of 'vicious circle' or *Teufelskreis* that Roper invokes – at least in the sense that psychological terror can be both irresistible and resisted by turns, but there is no reason to suspect further depth-psychological levels when Anna Maria seems to have been innocent, along with her family, and did her best to follow their martyr-like example.

Modern studies and first-hand accounts of torture also offer useful insights into the dynamics of interrogation. The testimony of modern torture survivors indicates that people resist interrogation under torture for as long as they can, and that the psychological effects of torture are varied but severe.[17] They also indicate that, while confessions may indeed be produced through a process of shaping and reshaping by both the prisoner and the interrogator, to suggest that prisoners experience this process as a sado-masochistic *game* is ludicrous. That is, they may well see their interrogators as sadists playing a game with their lives,[18] but not themselves as masochistic participants.

Survivors' accounts suggest various reasons for resistance and capitulation to interrogation. In one case, summarised in an essay by Felicity de Zulueta, a Tunisian man refused to cooperate with his interrogators despite being subjected to terrible torture. When asked by an interviewer why he did not cooperate, he responded that 'he wanted to preserve his dignity. He could not admit that people could be forced against their will.'[19] Others have described their feelings of intense fear and vulnerability, and explained that they confessed simply in order to stop the torture. A set of accounts by Burmese prisoners contains repeated stories of attempts to resist interrogation that falter or fail due to fear, confusion, and mental and physical exhaustion:

> 'When my physical situation deteriorated and I was unable to delay my interrogators any longer, I gave them some of the information they wanted.'[20]

> 'I became unsure of reality and my answers became inconsistent. Was I dreaming, or was all this really happening?'[21]

> 'I wasn't sure if I could take another round of torture. ... I was trembling with fear and I tried to come up with something that would get me out of the physical abuse.'[22]

'I was providing answers to their questions that I had previously resisted giving them. This was because I was weak and beginning to feel depressed.'[23]

There is nothing in such accounts to suggest that the authors believed their experiences were a game, or that they derived any sort of pleasure from them. For both men and women, being interrogated under torture was clearly deeply traumatic.

We have already noted that Lyndal Roper's psychosexual interpretation depends on female witches and male interrogators. It is undeniable that torture was and is very often sexualised, either through the application of pain to the genitals, rape, or the threat of rape. What may be forgotten is that women are not the only victims of sexual torture.[24] The following statements are from a female and a male Burmese torture survivor:

> One officer threatened that if I refused to confess I would lose my virginity. I was so frightened that I couldn't eat or sleep. If I confessed to the crime, although I had nothing to do with it, I would be sentenced to death. I couldn't decide what to do; I was in an impossible situation and I nearly went mad.[25]

> Suddenly, a guard kicked me behind my knee. I collapsed on the floor on my knees. When I tried to stand up, I was forced to lie on my back and I was handcuffed. The hood was still over my head and I was lying face down on the floor. Suddenly, my sarong was taken off. I wasn't wearing any underwear and my lower body was completely naked. ... I don't want to describe what followed because I don't even want to think about it. ... A voice broke the silence. 'Moe Aye, think carefully and tell us the truth. If you don't, we will make you a homosexual.' Someone then sat on top of me. Another took off my handcuffs, pulled both of my hands forward and handcuffed me again. I was about to be raped by another man. I was absolutely terrified as I expect anyone would be in such a situation.[26]

True and actual likeness of the newly built Evil-doers' House at Bamberg, built for the punishment and conversion of those who have turned away from and renounced God, of people who practise damnable magic and of evil-doers, begun in the current year 1627 in the month of June and finished in the following August.

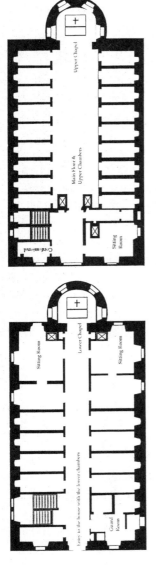

Sitting Room

Lower Chapel

Sitting Room

Entry to the house with the lower chambers

Guard Room

Upper Chapel

Main Floor & Upper Chambers

Sitting Room

Cartouches: citation from 3 Kings 9, 8-9 (= 1 Kings 9, 8-9), in Latin and German: 'And this house will become a ruin, every passer-by will be appalled and gasp [hiss] at the sight of it; and they will ask, "Why has the Lord so treated this land and this house?"' The answer will be, 'Because they forsook the Lord their God, who brought their forefathers out of Egypt, and clung to other gods, prostrating themselves before them and serving them; that is why the Lord has brought this great evil upon them.'

Legend (upper right):

C: A statue of Justice standing above the entry, under which is the verse: 'Having been warned, learn justice and do not despise God.' (Virgil, *Aeneid*, 6,620)

D: Label for the Chapel

E: The Torture Chamber

F: The stream that flows under the Torture Chamber

G: The Entrance to the Courtyard

2 The Bamberg *Hexenhaus* (witch-house), after a copper-plate engraving formerly in the Royal Library at Bamberg.

Both survivors express extreme fear and horror at the threat of rape (neither was actually raped), showing clearly that sexual torture and its effects are not suffered by women only.

We are not suggesting that torture lacks 'cultural mutability', or that modern categories may be imported wholesale into the past; indeed, we have argued precisely the opposite in our critique of Roper. Lisa Silverman has argued persuasively that there are important differences between the early modern context of torture, in which the application of pain in the pursuit of truth was both legal and 'partook of … a general cultural consent', and the modern context, in which torture is illegal and non-consensual.[27] Nevertheless, whatever the differences in culture, language and epoch between these survivors and early modern witches, they all had certain things in common: pain, resulting from the torture of their body; fear, even horror, of further or more brutal torture. And in all the cases we adduce here, they also have in common a fierce desire to resist the force being practised upon them – albeit with differing motivations: to preserve their soul, or the integrity of their personality, or their dignity, though these are, perhaps, different ways of referring to similar sorts of interiority.

A case study

The city of Bamberg was the site of one of the most infamous mass persecutions of witches in European history, with at least nine hundred burnings between 1624 and 1630.[28] Wolfgang Behringer has accounted for this surge by reference to massive crop failures, famines and epidemics in the period after 1624.[29] Johannes Junius, a *Bürgermeister* (variously burgomaster, alderman) of fifty-five, whose wife had been executed for witchcraft the previous year, was first examined on a charge of witchcraft on Wednesday, 28 June 1628, in what was for Bamberg a typical trial.[30] Junius was almost certainly held and tortured in the Bamberg *Hexenhaus*, which was purpose-built for this function in the summer of 1627 (see figure 2). It should be noted that there is no mention in the trial record or elsewhere that Junius was accused because of his wife's conviction.

At this first hearing, torture was not applied. Junius was accused by Dr Georg Adam Haan[31] of having frequented a gathering of witches in the electoral council chambers, where they ate and drank together. The accusation was, therefore, aimed directly at the top levels of urban society, and would seem to have been as much about civic politics, power and honour as about anything else. Junius denied this charge in its entirety, along with another concerning a 'witch-dance' in the *Hauptsmor* (Hamptsmoor) forest made by a woman named Elsse, wife or perhaps daughter of Hopffen ('Hopffens Elsse'). Having been left to think for two nights on the charges made against him by his supposed accomplices, Junius was again interrogated on Friday of that same week (30 June 1628). He was admonished to confess, but refused, and so was tortured, first by thumbscrews. He refused to confess anything, insisted that he had never denied God his Saviour or allowed himself to be baptised blasphemously, that is in a satanic parody of Christian baptism (see figure 3). The scribe wrote that he felt no pain. Under the intensified torture of leg-screws, Junius remained firm, confessing nothing. He professed to know nothing of the charges. He insisted again that he had never renounced God nor ever would, and that he still felt no pain. Subjected to the strappado, with his shoulders dislocated and his ligaments no doubt badly torn, Junius repeated that he had never renounced God and that God would not forsake him; he repeated that he knew nothing of witchcraft. Finally, Junius was stripped and examined, and a bluish mark like a clover leaf on his left side was pricked three times, but Junius was said to have felt no pain, and no blood flowed from it.

Both unnatural phenomena were believed to be signs of a witch: witches could not, according to current theories about witchcraft, feel ordinary pain, as they were protected from it by their pact with the Devil. Pain, as induced by torture, was meant to break through this layer of protection and help undo the bewitchment, leading a witch from the

3 Male and female witches; 'new mock baptism' of a male witch by a devil.

Devil to confession and reconciliation before salvific execution. It should be noted that although the court reporter claims that Junius felt no pain in the thumbscrews and leg-screws, Junius later wrote in a clandestine letter to his daughter that he suffered terrible agony under repeated hoistings and droppings (eight) via the strappado. This letter furnishes the core of our argument against Roper's readings of witches' confessions and their recantation.

Five further days of confinement in what we can legitimately presume to have been excruciating pain were followed by a hearing on Wednesday, 5 July, a mere week after Junius was first questioned. Without torture, the trial documents duly inform us, but under the urgent persuasion of the questioners, Junius 'at last begins and confesses'. Junius collapsed, furnishing the court with detailed accounts of his misdeeds and naming others who had been present, thereby

4 Male and female witches; male witch stepping on a cross as a sign of
   renouncing Christ.

accusing them of witchcraft as well. The details of his confession conform closely to the 'elaborated concept of witchcraft', as Wolfgang
Behringer has described it, that quasi-literary confabulation of satanic,
pagan and folk practice with utterly imaginary but quite ancient slan-
ders that had first coalesced in the *Malleus maleficarum* of 1487, but
did not reach its fully formed state until the sixteenth century. It is
important to note that Junius confessed to having renounced God in
Heaven and all the heavenly host by the formula 'I renounce God in
Heaven and his host, and will henceforth recognise the Devil as my
God' (see figures 4 and 5).[32] Given the insistence with which Junius
had, under torture, denied renouncing God, we can conclude that he
had been questioned closely and repeatedly about this item. The presence in the confession not only of a description of the act, but also of
the precise formula used, points to a carefully shaped and guided

5 Male and female witches standing in a magical circle to swear allegiance to the Devil.

process of question and response, which produced the final document that Junius ratified and confirmed in public on 6 August 1628, a full month after he 'at last began and confessed'. This is the key crime here, as in most other cases involving the 'elaborated concept'. There are also various local details and imps' names in the confession, but it follows the generic script very closely.

Remarkable by contrast for its candour and clear-sighted desperation, Junius' moving last letter to his daughter allows us to see at work a dynamic entirely different from that which Roper posited in her analysis of the witch trials she chose to examine. Junius wrote to his daughter Veronica after he had 'confessed'. Soldan and Heppe report that the letter survived because the judges kept it secret;[33] however, its presence in the file with the other documents does not prove this. On the contrary, had the letter been in the hands of the magistracy before

Junius' execution, he probably would not have been given the *coup de grâce* with a sword to spare him from being burned alive.[34] Junius dated the letter 24 July, approximately two weeks before his execution on 6 August; other internal evidence in the letter confirms this date. He declared his innocence movingly, in a rhetorically marked fashion that heightened the effect of the word *unschuldig*: 'Innocent I came into prison, innocent I was tortured, innocent I must die.' He related the circumstances of his first interrogations, which coincide precisely with the trial record: he was accused by the chancellor's son (Dr Georg Adam Haan, presumably) and Hopffens Elsse; he denied having eaten and danced with them and having renounced God. Thus far one is free to wonder to what extent he was repeating the official trial record, which may well have been read to him before 6 August, the date on which he confirmed his confession and was executed. However, after torture was applied, Junius' story diverges on a number of significant points from the court record. As we mentioned above, the court recorder claims that Junius felt no pain from the thumbscrews, leg-screws or pricking – a sure sign of a witch. Junius, however, tells a very different story:

> And then came – God in highest Heaven have mercy – the executioner, and put the thumbscrews on me, both hands bound together, so that the blood ran out at the nails and everywhere, so that for four weeks I could not use my hands, as you can see from the writing ... Thereafter they first stripped me, bound my hands behind me, and drew me up in the torture. Then I thought heaven and earth were at an end; eight times did they draw me up and let me fall again, so that I suffered horrible agony.[35]

Junius dates this to Friday, 30 June. This accords with the trial record, but Junius makes a careful protocol of the pain involved. One has the sense that he feels a strong need to justify himself in his daughter's eyes, and in the eyes of someone else again even more important to him: God.

Junius's letter makes a number of startling revelations and expresses his own motivations and sense of anguish at having confessed falsely, at having said that he had renounced God, at having accused others unjustly under compulsion. First of all, the executioner may well have been no sadistic dungeon-master but a frightened, bewildered functionary caught in the unstoppable judicial machinery that was consuming witches all around him. In fact, the executioner presented himself as a secret angel of mercy. He counselled Junius as follows:

> Sir, I beg you, for God's sake confess something, whether it be true or not. Invent something, for you cannot bear the torture which you shall suffer; and even if you bear it all, you still shall not escape, not even if you were a count, but one torture will follow another until you say you are a witch. Not before that will they let you go, as you may see by their trials, for one is just like another.[36]

It is highly improbable that any kind of tribunal should have instructed an executioner to counsel prisoners in this way. Furthermore, Junius begged his daughter to keep the letter secret because his jailers (*Wechter*) would be beheaded were it to be found. If we take the most probable reading of this advice, we must conclude that far from the executioner being forced by the accused witch to 'apply and reapply torture', here the executioner was begging his prisoner to avoid further torture by making *any* confession. Junius wrote that he was deeply anguished, day and night, about how to react to the executioner's advice, given that he would have to say that he was a witch, though he was not, and renounce God, though he had never done so.

The consequences of such a course of action were clearly, as becomes manifest in his other reasons for confessing and his discussion of his anguish over his confession, both the lives of others and the salvation of his own soul – not a sado-masochistic impulse to play Justine to the executioner's bargain-basement Marquis de Sade. Junius' solution is simple and shows how concerned he was with the state of his soul when the time came to face death. He would confess to avoid further (unnecessary) torture: 'I would surely be better to say it with mouth and words, even though I had not really done it; and afterwards I would confess it to the priest, and let those answer for it who compel me to do it.'[37]

By 'answer for it', Junius meant answer before God, since it was clear that the interrogators were not about to have to answer for it before anyone else. Faced with the inevitability of his death, Junius confessed, but claimed in his letter to have done so with mental reservations and to have planned to confess his false confession to the priest. There is one obligatory reason why he would confess it to the priest, and it was not primarily to unburden his conscience. Confession was by this time compulsory before receiving communion, but more importantly, it was necessary to confess all sins if one were to be absolved of them before it was too late, that is, before death. In Counter-Reformation Europe, this message was hammered home by obligatory weekly auricular confession and the adoption of the technology that made it practical: the confessional.[38] Junius then recounted, in terms that closely mirror those of the official trial record, how his questioners urged him to say that he had seen neighbours at the witch-gatherings, telling him to take a mental walk up and down the streets, through the market and into the castle. Junius made an effort to name as few people as possible. He was forced, however, to name his friend and colleague in the city government, Dietmeyer. Then they urged him to confess the crimes he had committed. When he said nothing, the court ordered him to be hoisted up again, so he said that he had been told to kill his children, but that he had been unable to do so and had killed a horse in their place. This did not satisfy the court, Junius related, so he said that he had taken a consecrated host and desecrated it, after which he was left in peace. The court had extracted enough evidence to convict him of diabolical witchcraft.

Junius summed up his experience by repeating the key ideas and the advice given him by the executioner:

Now dear child, here you have all my confession and [the record of] my trial, for which I must die. And they are sheer lies and inventions, so help me God. For I was forced to say all this through fear of the torture that was threatened beyond what I had already endured. For they never leave off with the torture till one confesses something; no matter how good he really is, he must be a witch. Nobody escapes, even if he is a count.[39]

After closing the letter formally, Junius adds:

Dear child, six witnesses have testified at the same time against me: the chancellor, his son, Neudecker, Zaner, Hoffmaisters Ursel and Hopffens Els[se], all falsely, through coercion as they have all told me, and begged me [to forgive them] for God's sake before their sentences were executed ... they knew nothing but good and nice things about me. They were forced to say it, just as I myself would experience.[40]

Both those who accused Junius and Junius himself were, therefore, most anxious at the very end of their life to apologise for their false confessions, to set the record straight with their fellows and before God. There was a so-called *Gnadenzettel*, a 'mercy note' among the documents pertaining to Junius' case: he was given the *coup de grâce* with a sword before being consigned to the flames.[41] His status and his confession, which he seems not to have recanted publicly, were probably the chief motivating factors in the decision to spare him death by burning. Despite this small mercy, Junius sees himself as a martyr and calls himself a martyr repeatedly: 'Sterbe also unschuldig und wie ein martirer' (I die innocent and as a martyr). He writes toward the end of the letter: 'I beg you for the sake of the Last Judgement, keep this letter under careful watch and pray for me as your father for a true martyr after my death ... You may boldly swear on my behalf that I am no witch (*Trudner*) but a martyr, and thus I die in readiness [for judgement].'[42]

These passages have been published in excerpts in a number of venues: by Friedrich Leitschuh in 1883,[43] by George Lincoln Burr, who published a translation in a small pamphlet titled *The Witch-Persecutions*,[44] by Soldan and Heppe in their polemical *Geschichte der Hexenprozesse* (Bauer's revised edition, 1911–12);[45] by Wolfgang Behringer in German;[46] and in the form of a rather stilted and highly abridged translation by Alan Kors and Edward Peters in 1972 in their classic English-language source book on witch-hunting.[47] We have appended a new translation of as much of the relevant portions of the text as was available to us. Junius' letter has been read previously as evidence for the injustice of witch trials; as proof that those accused generally confessed only under duress, especially torture; as proof that those accused of witchcraft, especially during epidemics of witch-hunting, did not need to have engaged in any traditional folk practices or 'magic' to be accused of witchcraft and executed for it; as proof that interrogators 'scripted' confessions for the accused and backed up these scripts with the threat of violence and actual violence. However, we can also read this document as proof that those who confessed to witchcraft often were forced to do so in the most brutal way; that 'collusion' in producing the confession was limited to lip-service; that a person like Junius retained complete mental reservations concerning the confession itself and intended to confess to confessing falsely to a priest; and that people such as those mentioned by Junius and Junius himself apologised to those they had falsely accused under torture.

Certainly Junius was not without agency in this process. On the contrary, he thought out and later recounted the mental process that led him to confess (in the light of the executioner's advice) against his will, but in order to avoid further and clearly useless suffering. He made a shrewd calculation that the experienced executioner who pleaded with him so sincerely was right that there was no escape in any case, and he chose a courageous and clever course of action. It is not unreasonable to suggest that his very human physicality, his inability to face further torture, led him to exercise his agency in this particular way. Roper, in seeing agency as irreducible and practically unfettered in the 'collusion' of a witch in producing her or his confession, disregards the vast power differential between interrogators, executioners and magistrates on the one hand, and anyone, including a burgomaster, or as Junius' executioner says, even a lord, who found himself charged with witchcraft – never mind a teenager, a middle-aged lying-in maid or a wet-nurse far from her own child – on the other. Junius is anxious over confessing to crimes that must, had they been true, have entailed the eternal damnation of his soul (renouncing God, the 'unforgivable sin'). The difference is that Junius is able to find a way to confess while saving his soul. Junius has an extremely powerful motivation: his own salvation, and probably that of others, was at stake.

Might we not say that those female witches whose confessions and retractions Roper analysed were moved by similar considerations? These women, we suggest, confessed and then withdrew their confessions in an agony of guilt at their wrong-doing and fear of its consequences, both for others falsely accused and for the salvation of their own soul. Once forced to confess again, as the logic of the 'elaborated concept' of diabolical witchcraft would have required them to do, they once again recanted as quickly as possible. Roper suggests that a witch who revokes her confession embarks on a horrifying 'game' of cat and mouse. Perhaps we can say that a witch who revokes her confession is asserting her self-understanding and self-definition, attempting to salvage her soul (or perhaps her 'Christian personality'), and not playing any other game at all.

Suzanne Gaudry, tried and executed for witchcraft at Ronchain in 1652, was interrogated on three separate occasions and tortured. The account of her first two interrogations suggests that she confessed freely to being a witch; that is, to being in the service of the Devil, to attending the 'nocturnal dance', and to practising *maleficium*. The only signs of resistance are her statements that she 'was frightened of being taken prisoner for the crime of witchcraft', that she had never abused the Holy Communion, and, in the second session, that her previous declaration was not true. At the end of each of these sessions, Gaudry signs a declaration of her various crimes.[48] At the third interrogation, the dynamic changes. We quote the exchange between Gaudry and her interrogators at length:

> The prisoner being led into the chamber, she was examined to know if things were not as she had said and confessed at the beginning of her imprisonment. – Answers no, and that what she has said was done so by force. ... Pressed to say the truth, that otherwise she would be subjected to torture, having pointed out to her that her aunt was burned for this same subject. – Answers that she is not a witch. ... Charged with having confessed to having made a horse die by means of a powder that the devil had given her. – Answers that she said it, but because she found herself during the inquisition pressed to say that she must have done some evil deed; and after several admonitions to tell the truth: She was placed in the hands of the officer ... , throwing herself on her knees, struggling to cry ... [s]aying at every moment that she is not a witch.[49]

Gaudry maintains her innocence throughout this session, which is interesting, for the court had learned that the 'peasants' who took Gaudry and another woman, Antoinette Lescouffre, to prison 'had persuaded them to confess in order to avoid imprisonment, and that they would be let go'.[50] This advice tends to explain why Gaudry confessed at first; perhaps she realised that her confessions were not helping her case after all, and so she adopted a different strategy in her third interrogation. The torture session shows Gaudry resisting, confessing, and recanting:

> The prisoner, before being strapped down, was admonished to maintain herself in her first confessions and to renounce her lover. – Said that she denies everything she has said, and that she has no lover. Feeling herself being strapped down, says that she is not a witch, while struggling to cry. Asked why she fled outside the village of Rieux. – Says that she cannot say it, that God and the Virgin Mary forbid her to; that she is not a witch.

And upon being asked why she confessed to being one, said that she was forced to say it. Told that she was not forced, that on the contrary she declared herself to be a witch without any threat. – Says that she confessed it and that she is not a witch, and being a little stretched [on the rack] screams ceaselessly that she is not a witch, invoking the name of Jesus and of Our Lady of Grace, not wanting to say any other thing. Asked if she did not confess that she had been a witch for twenty-six years. –Says that she said it, that she retracts it, crying Jésus-Maria, that she is not a witch. … Being more tightly stretched upon the torture-rack, urged to maintain her confessions. – Said that it was true that she is a witch and that she would maintain what she had said. … Interrogated as to what her lover was called. – Says that she said Petit-Grignon, then, being taken down [from the rack] says upon interrogation that she is not a witch and that she can say nothing. Asked if her lover has had carnal copulation with her, and how many times. – To that she did not answer anything; then, making believe that she was ill, not another word could be drawn from her. As soon as she began to confess, she asked who was alongside of her, touching her, yet none of those present could see anyone there. And it was noticed that as soon as that was said, she no longer wanted to confess anything.[51]

This witch cried out not to the Devil, but to Jesus and Mary – repeatedly. This parallels the invocations and imprecations of those martyred for their religious beliefs, as Brad Gregory has shown.[52]

It could be that witches such as Suzanne Gaudry, Regina Bartholome, Anna Ebeler, and Anna Maria Stadlin were not as clear in their minds as a legally experienced burgomaster about the contingent nature of a forced confession and one's ability to exculpate oneself from it by formal confession. To be sure, simple women knew all about confession if they were Catholics, but they might not have understood its mechanics as well as Junius did. If they were not Catholics, confession and absolution were not such simple matters for them, and as Gerald Strauss has shown, Protestants in the generations following

Luther often had no real idea of the mechanics of justification by faith alone, freely given grace, and the whole edifice of theology that made auricular confession theoretically unnecessary among Lutherans.[53]

If we see both Junius and women accused of witchcraft such as Anna Ebeler as working to save their souls, we are freed from any reason to use mental gymnastics to apply culture-bound, place-bound and time-bound theories about human sexuality, or even the much-discussed links between *eros* and *thanatos*, to explain their behaviour. These accused witches and recanters may well have been concerned first and foremost with the state of their soul, their injury of others, and their own salvation. This definition of personal integrity might not correspond closely to contemporary occidental understandings of personal identity, self-knowledge and the like. However, the integrity of the soul as regards salvation was crucial – as studies such as Brad Gregory's book on martyrdom, *Salvation at Stake*, are proving – to the self-understanding of early modern Christians in life-and-death confrontations with 'capital justice'.[53] Men and women might have negotiated these confrontations differently, but their motivations, as they expressed them, were fundamentally the same. The soul in peril, not the *female* psyche, seems to have been the central concern to both accused and accusers. When torture is applied to save souls (rather than to play games), then not only the tortured *female* body, but also the tortured *human* body, the receptacle of the human soul, deserves attention in studies of witch trials. Studies that focus on the trials of female witches perform the vital and much-neglected task of illuminating and recovering the role of women in history; however, such gender-specific studies often occult the gender-inclusive nature of witch-hunting and ideas about witches.

Notes

1 See e.g. Naess, 'Norway: The criminological context', 375. 'Great pain was inflicted on the accused witches and sorcerers. The pastors were present and asked the prisoners to confess to diabolism. Naturally they did in the end.'

2 See Ira Cohen, 'Structuration theory and social *praxis*', *Social Theory Today*, eds. Anthony Giddens and Jonathan Turner (Stanford: Stanford University Press, 1987), 291, 300; Margaret S. Archer, *Being Human: The Problem of Agency* (Cambridge: Cambridge University Press, 2000); George W. Harris, *Agent-Centered Morality: An Aristotelian Alternative to Kantian Internalism* (Berkeley: University of California Press, 1999); John Martin Fisher, *The Metaphysics of Free Will: An Essay on Control* (Cambridge: Blackwell, 1994).

3 'The elaborated concept' is a conglomerate of: 1) the Devil's pact (and apostasy); 2) a sexual relationship with the Devil; 3) the possibility of aerial flight to 4) the witches' sabbath to worship the Devil; 5) maleficent witchcraft. Behringer, *Witchcraft Persecutions in Bavaria*, 13–14.

4 Lisa Silverman has noted that research on torture faces a very similar problem: 'Torture is always at the center of an epistemological crisis because it always forces us to reconsider the relationship between coercion and truth, between free will and evidence.' *Tortured Subjects: Pain, Truth, and the Body in Early Modern France* (Chicago and London: Chicago University Press, 2001), 10.

5 On the closely related subject of writing about early modern torture, Lisa Silverman argues that historians, by representing the testimony of early modern torture victims 'as composed of deliberate lies', have a tendency to represent torture victims as if they were fully endowed with agency, volition, and rationality'. She observes also that literary critics, on the other hand, represent modern torture victims 'as absolute victims', innocent and rendered so completely 'passive through pain that they cannot articulate this innocence'. *Tortured Subjects*, 86–87.

6 'Witchcraft and fantasy', 202.

7 Oxford: Clarendon Press, 1989.

8 That this version of the theory of agency owes a good deal to classical liberal concepts of free will and autonomous choice that both Marxists and Tories can agree to despise causes Roper no hesitation.

9 Roper, 'Oedipus and the Devil', *Oedipus and the Devil*, 226–248.

10 *Ibid.*, 227.

11 Roper, 'Witchcraft and fantasy', esp. 203 ff.

12 *Ibid.*, 207ff.

13 *Ibid.*, 205.

14 *Ibid.*, 205–206.

15 Porter, 'Witchcraft and magic', 249.

16 Wilhelm Gottlieb Soldan and Henriette Heppe; Max Bauer, ed., *Geschichte der Hexenprozesse*, 2 vols. (Munich: Georg Müller, 1911–12),

vol. 2, 324. A reprint is available: Darmstadt: Wissenschaftliche Buchgesellschaft/ Hanau: Müller & Kiepenheuer, 1972.

17 See Duncan Forrest, 'Methods of torture and its effects', *A Glimpse of Hell: Reports on Torture Worldwide,* ed. Duncan Forrest (New York: New York University Press, 1996), 104–121: 117.

18 Various studies have suggested that torturers are not, generally speaking, sadists; evidence indicates that torturers are made, not born. See e.g. Ronald D. Crelinsten and Alex P. Schmid, eds., *The Politics of Pain: Torturers and their Masters* (Boulder, CO: Westview, 1995).

19 Felicity de Zulueta, 'The torturers', *A Glimpse of Hell,* 87–103: 87. Among other things, the man was beaten with pipes and sticks; his skin was torn from his nails and between his toes and fingers, then burned; his moustache was torn out; and one of his torturers urinated in his mouth.

20 Ma Su Su Mon, 'At the mercy of the beast', *Tortured Voices: Personal Accounts of Burma's Interrogation Centers,* ed. Aung Moe Htet (Bangkok: All Burma Students' Democratic Front, 1998), 25–30: 28.

21 Win Naing Oo, 'In the flames of evil', *Tortured Voices,* 31–48: 39.

22 Tin Win Aung, 'Into the darkness', *Tortured Voices,* 58–67: 66.

23 Ning Kyaw, 'Like water in their hands', *Tortured Voices,* 106–122: 120.

24 Granted, women are more likely to be victimised in this way, and the risk of impregnation is specific to women. For a brief overview of sexual torture, see Mike Jempson, 'Torture worldwide', *A Glimpse of Hell,* 46–86. On the concept of rape as torture and as a war crime, see Rhonda Copelon, 'Surfacing gender: Reconceptualizing crimes against women in time of war', *The Women and War Reader,* eds. Lois Ann Lorentzen and Jennifer Turpin (New York and London: New York University Press, 1998), 63–79.

25 Ma Su Su Mon, 'At the mercy of the beast', 29.

26 Moe Aye, 'A dialogue with the Devil', *Tortured Voices,* 68–99: 84.

27 Silverman, *Tortured Subjects,* 20–21.

28 See Wolfgang Behringer, *Witchcraft Persecutions in Bavaria,* 96–97; esp. 224–229; 311, 314: end of Bamberg persecution in 1630; see also Behringer, 'Witchcraft studies in Austria, Germany and Switzerland', *Witchcraft in Early Modern Europe,* 64–95: mention of Bamberg on p. 85. On the end of the Bamberg witch-panic, see Britta Gehm, *Die Hexenverfolgungen im Hochstift Bamberg und das Eingreifen des Reichshofrates zu ihrer Beendigung* (Hildesheim: Georg Olm, 2000), as well as the more technical study by Peter Oestmann, *Hexenprozesse am Reichskammergericht* (Cologne: Böhlau, 1997). See also P. Wittman, 'Die Bamberger Hexenjustiz 1595–1631', *Archiv für das katholische Kirchenrecht* 50 (1883), 177–223. Soldan and Heppe, *Hexenprozesse,* note

that a news pamphlet approved by the archiepiscopal authorities at Bamberg put the total for the entire region under the control of Bamberg (*Stift*) at around 900 (vol. 2, 17).

29 Behringer, *Witchcraft Persecutions in Bavaria*, 94ff.

30 The records were in the 'municipal library' at Bamberg. The three-part trial of Junius is quite typical for Bamberg: Soldan and Heppe, *Hexenprozesse*, vol. 2, 14, citing Johann Diefenbach, *Der Hexenwahn vor und nach der Glaubensspaltung* (Mainz, 1886), 132; photomechanical reprints Leipzig: Zentralantiquariat der DDR, 1979; Wiesbaden: Fourier, 1988.

31 The entire Haan family and their servants were destroyed after *Kanzler* Dr Georg Haan (a functionary of the *Hochstift* Bamberg) began to doubt the correctness of the accusations and trials in the mounting witch-panic. His trial lasted from December 1627 to July 1628. Dr Georg Adam Haan was his son (tried 27 May to 13 July 1628); Junius was accused by the latter and drawn into the wake of the Haan trials. The only study of the Haan trials is Andrea Renczes, *Wie löscht man eine Familie aus? Eine Analyse Bamberger Hexenprozesse* (Pfaffenweiler: Centaurus-Verlagsgesellschaft, 1992). This is a careful archival treatment but the author's interpretations and conclusions are of limited value.

32 Behringer, *Witchcraft Persecutions in Bavaria*, 218: The 'central spiritual crime' of the elaborated concept of witchcraft was the pact with the Devil and renunciation of God. It was characteristic of Catholic views that intercourse with the Devil, witches' flights, Sabbaths and sorcery were also held to be real, not merely diabolical fantasies, as claimed by critics, including many Protestants.

33 Soldan and Heppe, *Hexenprozesse*, vol. 2, 6.

34 Soldan and Heppe, *Hexenprozesse*, vol. 2, 13–14. Kors and Peters simply assume that the letter was 'smuggled out of prison to his daughter' (*Witchcraft in Europe*, 253) without questioning Soldan.

35 Und da kam leider, Gott erbarm es im höchsten himmel der hencker und hat mir den Daumenstock angelegt, bede hende zusamen gebunden, daß das blut zu den negeln heraußgangen und allenthalben daß ich die hendt in 4 Wochen nicht brauch koennen, wie du da auß dem schreiben seh kannst. … Darnach hat man mich erst außgezogen, die hendt uf den Rücken gebunden und uf die höhe in der Fulter gezogen. Da dachte ich, himmel und erden ging under, haben mich achtmahl auffgezogen, und wieder fallen lassen, daß ich unselig schmerzen empfan (7–8).

36 Herr, ich bitt euch umb gotteswillen, bekennt etwas, es sey gleich war oder nit. Erdenket etwas, dann ir könnt die marter nicht ausstehen, die man

euch anthut, vnd wann ir sie gleich alle ausstehet, so kompt ir doch niht hinaus, wann Ir gleich ein graff weret, sondern fangt ein marter wider auf die andre an, bis ir saget, ir seyt ein Truttner, und sagt, eher, eher niht dann lest man euch zufrieden, wie denn auß allen iren urtheylen zu sehen, daß eins wie das ander gehet (8–9).

37 Es war ja besser, ich sagt es nur mit dem mauhl und worten, und hette es aber im werck niht getan, sollte es danach beychten und es die verant-worten lassen, die mich dazu nötigen (9).

38 See, most recently, Wietse de Boer, *The Conquest of the Soul: Confession, Discipline and Public Order in Counter-Reformation Milan*, Studies in Medieval and Reformation Thought 84 (Leiden: Brill, 2001).

39 Nun, hertzliebes kindt, da hastu alle meine Aussag und verlauf, darauf ich sterben muß und seint lautter lüg und erdichte sach, so war mir gott helff. Dann dieses habe ich alles auß forcht der ferner angetrohenen marter uber die schon zuvor außgestandene Marter sag muß. Denn sie lassen nicht mit den martern nach, biß man etwas sagt, er sey so fromm als er wolle, so muß er ein trudener sein. Kompt auch keiner herauß, wenn er gleich ein graf wär (11).

40 Liebes Kindt 6 haben auf einmahl auf mich bekennt, als: der Cantzler, sein sohn, Neudecker, Zaner, Hoffmaisters Ursel und Hopffens Els alle falsch auß zwang wie sie alle gesagt, und mir umb Gotteswillen eher sie gerichtet abgebetten ... worden sie wissen nichts alß liebs und guts von mir. Sie hetten es sag muß, wie ich selbsten erfahren werde [...] (8). Cf. the faulty translation in Alan C. Kors and Peters, *Witchcraft in Europe 1100–1700* 'just as I myself was'; this is reported speech set before his torture.

41 Soldan and Heppe, *Hexenprozesse*, vol. 2, 13–14.

42 Ich bitte dich um des jüngsten gerichts willen, halt dies schreiben in guter Hut und bet für mich als dein vatter für ein rechten merterer nach meinem tode ... Das darfst künlich für mich schwören daß ich kein trudner son-dern ein mertirer bin und sterb hiemit gefast (12).

43 Friedrich Leitschuh, *Beiträge zur Geschichte des Hexenwesens in Franken* (Bamberg: Hübscher, 1883), 49ff.

44 George Lincoln Burr, *The Later Persecutions*. Translations and Reprints from the Original Sources of European History, vol. 3 no. 4 (Philadelphia: n.p., 1897).

45 Soldan and Heppe *Hexenprozesse*, vol. 2: Junius' letter to his daughter in German (original orthography) and a facsimile of the first sheet, 6–12.

46 Wolfgang Behringer, ed., *Hexen und Hexenprozesse* (Munich: dtv, 1988), 305–310.

47 Kors and Peters, *Witchcraft in Europe 1100–1700*.

48 *Ibid.*, 266–271.

49 *Ibid.*, 272–274.
50 *Ibid.*, 272.
51 *Ibid.*, 274–275.
52 Gerald Strauss, *Luther's House of Learning: Indoctrination of the Young in the German Reformation* (Baltimore: Johns Hopkins University Press, 1978).
53 See Brad S. Gregory, *Salvation at Stake: Christian Martyrdom in Early Modern Europe* (Cambridge, MA: Harvard University Press, 1999).

4

LITERALLY UNTHINKABLE?
DEMONOLOGICAL DESCRIPTIONS OF
MALE WITCHES

The previous chapters presented challenges to generalisations about male witches. The next two chapters follow a similar approach to conventional perspectives on the demonological treatment of witchcraft and gender. Through the examination of witchcraft theorists' descriptions of male witches, we aim to show that, just as with the 'real life' cases, modern scholars' views do not take sufficient account of the complexity of early modern learned theories about witches.

The sources for this discussion are demonological treatises published in the fifteenth, sixteenth and seventeenth centuries. The body of witchcraft literature is much too large to permit a complete survey; there is, however, a smaller group of works that could be considered canonical, at least from the perspective of contemporary scholarship. This 'canon' includes Jean Bodin's *De la demonomanie des sorciers*, Johannes Nider's *Formicarius*, and the *Malleus maleficarum*, which occupies pride of place within the literature as possibly the most (in)famous treatise of them all. In this chapter, we present data compiled from ten of these canonical works, as well as a brief discussion of demonological illustrations.

Demonological literature has received relatively little scholarly attention, especially compared with the number of published studies that focus on non-literary, archival materials such as court records and pamphlets. Although witchcraft scholars refer frequently to the *Malleus* and its fellow witchcraft treatises, they rarely engage in sustained analyses of these works. One reason for this neglect is the social-historical emphasis on non-elite subjects; another is the generally poor reputation that demonological texts have as documents of barbarity, superstition, and irrationality. H.R. Trevor-Roper, for example, said of them that

> To read these encyclopedias of witchcraft is a horrible experience. Each seems to outdo the last in cruelty and absurdity. Together they insist that every grotesque detail of demonology is true, that scepticism must be stifled, that sceptics and lawyers who defend witches are themselves witches, that all witches, 'good' or 'bad', must be burnt, that no excuse, no extenuation is allowable ... When we read these monstrous treatises, we find it difficult to see their authors as human beings.[1]

The historiographical tide is shifting, and several monograph studies of demonological works and the contexts in which they were produced are now available.[2] There are also essay collections and several individual articles dealing with this material.[3] In general, however, demonological literature has not attracted much scholarly attention, and within the historiographical genre of demonological studies, research has focused on the links between demonology and the rise and decline of witch-hunting.

This approach often takes the form of summarising and criticising the arguments of individual authors. For example, Christopher Baxter's essay on Johann Weyer's *De praestigiis daemonum* consists mainly of an evaluation of Weyer's effectiveness in opposing witch-hunting. Baxter argues (against Trevor-Roper) that Weyer's work is actually 'a protest against policies of toleration'; if only, Baxter implies, Weyer had been more rational, he could have achieved the proper goal of arguing for tolerance.[4] Baxter remarks in his conclusion that 'Weyer's writings badly misfired as a defence of witches', in part because 'his simplistic theological commitment prevent[ed] him from pushing through to a logical and systematic re-interpretation of traditional attitudes an unprecedentedly diverse, though individually unoriginal, range of arguments for tolerance.'[5]

Although there is genuine debate over the role of demonology in the development and decline of witch-hunting,[6] interpretations of demonological conceptions of gender and witchcraft are remarkably uniform in their concentration on what witchcraft theorists had to say about women. There is some disagreement over how representative or extreme demonological misogyny was (see chapter 1's discussion of Stuart Clark's views), but the focus on women itself has not been challenged. This is understandable, to a point. There is no denying that the major demonological treatises of the period, both those that advocated witch-hunting and those that opposed it, accepted that most witches were women. For example, in their explanation of why more women than men were witches, the much-quoted Institoris and Sprenger incorporated many citations of classical, biblical and medieval authorities. One of these, a citation of Valerius' letter to Rufinus, reads: 'Chimeram mulierem esse nescis sed scire debes quod monstrum illud triforme insigni venustetur facie leonis olentis maculetur ventre capre virulente cauda vippere armetur. vult dicere. quod est aspectus eius pulcer. tactus fetidus. conuersatio mortifera.'[7] Most modern readers will be more familiar with Montague Summers' translation: 'You do not know that woman is the Chimaera, but it is good that you should know it; for that monster was of three forms; its face was that of a radiant and noble lion, it had the filthy belly of a goat, and it was armed with the virulent tail of a viper. And he means that a woman is beautiful to look upon, contaminating to the touch, and deadly to keep.'[8] When one reads such statements, it is not difficult to see why modern scholars, especially feminists, have been fascinated by demonological treatments of women.

The problem is not that scholars have paid attention to the early modern demonological discourse about women and witchcraft; it is that they have given their attention *only* to the discourse about women, as if early modern authors said nothing about men as perpetrators of witchcraft. This is not because scholars are unaware of the presence of male witches within demonological texts. Several historians, all of whom were writing from a feminist perspective, have noticed that early modern authors discussed male witches. For example, Anne Barstow mentions that Henri Boguet, chief judge of St. Cloud in Franche-Comté and author of the *Discours des sorciers*, said that male and female witches were equally addicted to the carnal pleasures offered by the Devil.[9] Carol Karlsen remarks on the language used by early modern authors: 'While authors of theological descriptions of witchcraft sometimes employed female pronouns when speaking generally about witches, more commonly they used the "generic" male.'[10] Susanna Burghartz, while arguing that 'a concentration on women as witches is certainly evident' in Nider's *Formicarius*, says that 'all the same, Nider's examples of witches include an astonishing number of men.'[11]

The critical point here is that this is *all* that these authors have to say about the inclusion of male witches in early modern texts: they mention it once, then never bring it up again. In Barstow's case, the reference to Boguet's 'even-handedness' is not even in the main body of the text; it is buried in an appendix. Burghartz's astonishment at finding a number of male witches in the *Formicarius* is particularly telling. Burghartz knows from reading Richard Kieckhefer's study of medieval European witch trials that in the mid-fifteenth century, when the *Formicarius* was composed, a significant proportion (32 per cent) of witches were male, and she knows that 'it was always possible to prosecute men for witchcraft'.[12] Why, then, the astonishment? Her reaction to the *Formicarius* indicates a strong degree of conditioning by a historiography and ideology that is always already committed to a particular way of reading demonological texts. Modern readers appear to assume that there will be no surprises in the gendered discourse of these texts, and then seem unable to address them except in deceptively casual, throwaway remarks.

Even Stuart Clark, whom one might expect to engage with male witches in demonology, does not. Indeed, he does not mention their textual existence at all, despite his careful reading of the early modern gendering of witchcraft. Like the other historians discussed above, he is well aware that many witches were men. He evinces no interest in this fact, however, preferring to focus on why witches 'were *conceived* to be women.'[13] Clark suggests two points that bear on the subject of male witches: first, that there was a 'lack of conformity between demonological theory and the actual sexual breakdown in those witchcraft prosecutions where men made up a significant minority or even a substantial portion of those accused.' Second, he states that 'it was literally unthinkable', at a demonological level, 'that witches should be male,' because early modern theorists were committed to a hierarchically structured binary framework in which femaleness was associated with evil.[14] In effect, Clark argues not only that there was a conceptual affinity between women and witchcraft, but also that there was a conceptual *barrier* between men and witchcraft.

Clark's conclusions are similar to those of Eric Wilson, whose Cambridge dissertation is the first modern study in English of the *Malleus maleficarum*. Wilson devotes a chapter to the issue of women in the *Malleus*, but never once refers to the fact that the text's authors also wrote about men who were witches, or to their use of both *maleficus* and *malefica*. He notes that 'the text even employs the feminine form of the Latin word for witch ... rather than the more commonly employed masculine.'[15] Wilson knows full well that many witches were male, and he states his agreement with Christina Larner that witchhunting was sex-related rather than sex-specific;[16] nevertheless, he concludes that there was a 'necessary relationship between women and witchcraft'.[17]

Both Clark and Wilson suggest that early modern demonology was sex-specific and thus different from witchcraft prosecutions, which were merely sex-related. This position is actually more extreme than that of most feminist scholars, who at least hint that demonological conceptions of gender and witchcraft were not always tidy and coherent. It is not, perhaps, completely surprising that it is the feminists who have shown more sensitivity. Their primary purpose, generally speaking, is to explain the preponderance of women in witch trials; they examine the contents of demonological treatises for evidence of systematic misogyny, and are less interested in the treatises as worthy objects of study in and of themselves.

In contrast, scholars such as Clark and Wilson are interested in recovering demonological texts from the historiographical neglect into which they had fallen. Clark and Wilson are not unsympathetic to feminist concerns, and treat the issue of women and witchcraft seriously; however, their underlying concern is with demonstrating the logic and coherence of early modern demonology. This leads Clark and Wilson to exclude male witches from their discussions because they are unable to incorporate them without subverting their intellectual-historical agenda of making the texts respectably coherent.[18]

We have emphasised the exclusion of male witches from analyses of witchcraft literature so strongly because it is simply not credible that scholars working with these texts (at least those working with original-language editions) do not know about them.[19] As table 2 shows, it was not at all uncommon for early modern authors from the fifteenth to the seventeenth century to refer to witches in both masculine and feminine terms. Furthermore, certain treatises included illustrations of both male and female witches, and individual male witches are described in many tracts. It is only by deciding, a priori, that male witches are insignificant that one could treat early modern demonology as sex-specific.

Texts

When we 'discovered' that Heinrich Institoris and Jacob Sprenger referred to witches in both masculine and feminine terms, one of our first questions concerned the relative frequency of the masculine usage. Just how often did these and other authors employ masculine forms when discussing witches, and did they do so more frequently than they used feminine forms? Modern commentary on the language of demonology (in a philological sense) is sketchy, and we found nothing that answered our specific questions about the *Malleus* satisfactorily. For example, Sigrid Brauner offers a brief discussion of the use of *maleficus* and *malefica* in the *Malleus*, but her assertion that Institoris and Sprenger 'use the male plural form *malefici* for sorcerers in general but reserve the female form *malefica* for the modern witch' is mistaken.[20] In 1.1, Institoris and Sprenger refer to 'moderni malefici' specifically: 'Tertium etiam sane intelligere expedit cum moderni malefici sepius ope demonum transformantur in lupos et alias bestias.' (And third, it is indeed useful to understand how modern [contemporary] witches [male; and possibly female, according to convention] are often transformed by the power of a demon into wolves and other beasts.)[21]

Our approach to this problem was fairly simple: we counted the number of times the authors used masculine and feminine terms for witches. Our aim in tabulating this information about linguistic gendering is to challenge Clark's notion that early modern witchcraft theorists were incapable of imagining that witches could be male, on the grounds that language choices are not accidental and that early modern authors must have meant to use both masculine and feminine terms. If they were capable of representing witches as male, it follows that they were also capable of conceptualising male witches – otherwise, their language would make no sense.

For this purpose, an extensive survey of the very large corpus of witchcraft literature is unnecessary. A small sample of major texts is sufficient to show that witchcraft theorists had no difficulty representing witches as male. The texts were selected partly on the basis of availability in original-language editions, but also for their status as well-known treatises with which most historians will have some familiarity. There is a certain degree of uniformity, in that nine of the texts are 'pro' witchhunting, the exception being Friedrich Spee's *Cautio criminalis*.

Early modern terminology for magic and magic-users varied considerably, even within elite discourse. The terms *maleficus* and *malefica* were quite common, but so were the terms *saga*, *sortilegus*, and *veneficus*, to list only a few. The sample texts employ several different terms.

In our tabulation, we were most interested in parallel forms, such as *maleficus/malefica* and *sorcier/sorcière*, but we have also enumerated other terms so as to give a reasonable indication of the relative frequency of references to male and female witches. In general, words that appear only once or twice, or have a specialist meaning, such as *necromanticus* or *pythonissa*, have not been included in the tabulation.

The *Formicarius*, *Malleus maleficarum*, *De laniis*, and *Flagellum haereticorum* use *maleficus* and *malefica* almost exclusively. Daneau employs a variety of terms in *De veneficis*: *veneficus* (24), *sortilegus* (16), *maleficus* (4), and *sortiarius* (140) for male witches; *venefica* (1), *saga* (1), and *satanae* (86) for female witches. In the *Tractatus*, Binsfeld prefers *maleficus* and *saga* (30), but also uses *malefica* (17). Rémy's *Daemonolatreia* uses *sortilegus* (24) and *saga* (34) most often for male and female witches respectively, but also *maleficus* (6) and *malefica* (5), and refers to a *sortilega* once. Bodin and de Lancre employ *sorcier* and *sorcière*. In *Cautio criminalis*, Spee uses *maleficus* for male witches and *saga* for female witches. The figures given represent the sum totals of both plural and singular forms.

Where possible, we have used first editions of these treatises, as indicated in the endnotes to the table; however, first editions have not always been available, which raises the issue of textual stability. As Adrian Johns has argued, contra Elizabeth Eisenstein, early modern printed texts were not inherently stable, and the fixity of print in the period has been much exaggerated.[22] There is no reason to assume that demonological treatises were any less susceptible to piracy and printers' errors or emendations than, say, Galileo's *Sidereus nuncius*, whose later editions featured corrupted images.[23]

Indeed, comparisons of two editions of the *Formicarius*[24] and twenty-one copies (sixteen different editions) of the *Malleus maleficarum*[25] reveal that demonological treatises were not completely stable texts. For example, the first lines of both treatises contain textual variants. In the 1480 edition of the *Formicarius*, book 5 begins: '*Ultimo loco* per libellum quintum sub formicarum proprietatibus de maleficis &

eorum decepcionibus *concludere restat*'.[26] The same line of the 1669 edition reads: '*Nunc* per libellum quintum sub formicarum proprietatibus de maleficis & eorum deceptionibus *agere placet*.'[27] The first line of the 1487 *Malleus maleficarum* reads: 'Utrum asserere maleficos esse sit a deo catholicum quod eius oppositum pertinaciter *defendere* omnino sit hereticum.'[28] In several later editions, the word *defendere* is replaced by either *asserere* or *offendere*.[29]

This textual variation suggests a need for caution when assessing the reception of demonological works. Different editions were highly unlikely to be identical. Historians of witchcraft need to develop an awareness of this instability. Certain variations call into question broad assertions about the reception of the *Malleus* and other texts: for instance, despite some claims to the contrary, not every edition of the *Malleus* included a copy of the papal bull *Summis desiderantes*.[30] On the other hand, the gendered terminology of the *Formicarius* and *Malleus* is remarkably stable. We have detected only one variant, which is found in the *Formicarius*. In book 5, chapter 3, the 1669 edition has *maleficarum* where the 1480 edition has *maleficorum*.[31] Granted, our variants search has been limited; however, we are reasonably confident that this particular feature of demonological treatises was not affected significantly by textual instability, and that the textual (grammatical) gendering of witches was consistent during the early modern period.

Counting words may seem to be a strange way of uncovering textual meaning. We are more accustomed to what we might think of as qualitative approaches to language, in which we puzzle over the meanings and intentions of specific language choices; we do not usually quantify those choices. In this case, however, quantification provides a means of introducing some methodological rigour to the discussion of gender and witchcraft. Given the hegemonic status of conventional readings of demonology, it would be extremely difficult to make the case for the inclusion of male witches as significant subjects without some kind of hard data.

The data presented in table 2 are not meant to establish definitively the universal patterns of gendered language usage in early modern demonology. However, even a rough approximation of the complexity of demonological concepts of witchcraft and gender is an important step toward breaking out of our own tendency to essentialise past ideas.

Table 2: *References to witches in demonological texts*

Edition	Author	Text	Masculine	Feminine
1480[32]	Nider	*Formicarius*, Bk. 5	47	13
1487[33]	Institoris & Sprenger	*Malleus maleficarum*	197	453
1489[34]	Molitor	*De laniis*	35	44
1580[35]	Bodin	*De la demonomanie des sorciers*	820	399
1581[36]	Jacquier	*Flagellum haereticorum*	40	3
1581[37]	Daneau	*De veneficis*	174	88
1591[38]	Binsfeld	*Tractatus de confessionibus*	157	47
1595[39]	Rémy	*Daemonolatreia*	30	40
1613[40]	de Lancre	*Tableau de L'Inconstance*	335	296
1632[41]	Spee	*Cautio criminalis*	41	258

These figures represent a reduction of complex usage patterns to a simple dichotomy between masculine and feminine references. Speaking broadly, the references to witches in demonological texts may be divided into 'abstract' and 'concrete' categories. Abstract references concern the characteristics and abilities of witches as a 'species'. For example, in the first chapter of book 5 of the *Formicarius*, the Piger asks the Theologian ('Theologus'; the *Formicarius* is written as a dialogue between these two speakers) about witches and their relationship with demons: 'Desidero igitur noscere Primo quot modis & qualiter malefici & supersticiosi sibique similes reguntur equitantur & dementantur per demones.'[42] (I desire therefore to know, first, in how many ways and by what right witches and the superstitious and those like them are ruled, ridden and driven mad by demons.) Abstract references are ordinarily plural, and very often masculine. Nider, for instance, always uses the masculine when referring to witches in the abstract. Some abstract references are singular, and are masculine or feminine depending on the author and context. In the *Malleus maleficarum*, singular abstract references are usually feminine, but the section concerning whether the Devil and witch must cooperate in order to perform *maleficium* begins: 'An catholicum sit asserere quod ad effectum maleficialem semper habeat demon cum malefico concurrere vel quod vnus sine altero vt demon sine malefico vel econuerso talem possit producere.'[43] (Whether it is orthodox to affirm that in order to achieve an act of sorcery a demon must always work together with a witch, or that one without the other, for instance a demon without a witch or vice versa, is able to produce such an act.) In this passage, the abstract witch is referred to in the masculine ablative singular form *malefico*.

Concrete references describe actual witches, usually in connection with a trial. Concrete references are either masculine or feminine, singular or plural, depending on the context. Early modern authors never, to our knowledge, confuse the gender of their concrete references. Whether a woman or a man is the subject of discussion, the term used to describe that individual always agrees in grammatical gender with their biological sex. We have found no instance of a particular male witch described in grammatically feminine terms, or vice versa.

It is important to distinguish between abstract and concrete language because such references have different, but related, heuristic values. Abstract references suggest the degree to which early modern witchcraft theorists conceptualised witches as inherently gendered. It is an imperfect measure of such conceptualisation: abstract masculine references were in all likelihood meant to include females, and in any case grammatical gender cannot always be read as indicative of 'actual' gender. For example, several masculine Latin nouns with feminine end-ings – *agricola*, *nauta*, and *poeta*, to list a few – refer to traditionally masculine occupations. On the other hand, the fact that different forms existed for witches suggests that the use of a masculine noun, such as *maleficus*, was not purely a matter of grammatical convention. Conceptual flexibility was built into the languages of early modern witchcraft theory.

The texts do provide clues as to how their authors were using lan-guage. In the *Formicarius*, Nider uses the masculine plural *malefici* unless referring specifically to female witches. His statement that Peter of Como burned many witches of both sexes ('multos vtriusque sexus incineravit maleficos') suggests that such usage is inclusive of men and women.[44] Here, *maleficos* clearly means both men and women. This is actually a concrete reference, but it is reasonable to assume that his abstract references are also inclusive, since he devotes a later chapter to the special wickedness of women. Nider does not say 'maleficos et maleficas'; presumably, this would have been considered redundant.

For the most part, Jean Bodin follows Nider's pattern. He uses mas-culine plurals and singulars unless female witches are the specific sub-ject of reference. For instance, Bodin begins his first chapter: 'Sorcier est celuy qui par moyens Diaboliques sciemment s'efforce de paruenir a quelque chose.'[45] (A witch is one who knowingly tries to do something by diabolical means.) This use of the masculine singular in a chapter devoted to defining what a witch is constructs the witch as male, not female – at least in a linguistic sense. Similarly, Pierre de Lancre begins his *Tableau de L'Inconstance* with a chapter on the inconstancy of demons, in which (abstract) witches are referred to in the masculine. He says, for instance, that 'A la vérité les Démons ont quelque certaine légèreté, laquelle fait qu'ils peuvent aisément et en un moment surnager et enfoncer, et en communiquer les moyens aux Sorciers non pas que de la on doive tirer une preuve certaine et infaliable qu'ils sont Sorciers.'[46] (In truth, demons have a certain inconstancy, which makes them able easily and in a moment to float and to sink, and to communicate the means of doing so to witches, not that one should draw from this certain and infallible proof that they are witches [i.e. in a swimming test].)

The linguistic patterns of the *Malleus maleficarum* are far more complex than in the works of Nider, Bodin and de Lancre. Institoris and Sprenger begin with masculine references, but gradually switch to an almost exclusive use of feminine forms for abstract discussions. This linguistic transformation is not smooth. Institoris and Sprenger explain that the heresy of witches ought to be described in feminine, not masculine terms, because most witches are women: 'Plura hic deduci possent sed intelligentibus satis apparet non mirum quod plures reperiuntur infecti heresi maleficorum mulieres quam viri. Unde et consequenter heresis dicenda est non maleficorum sed maleficarum vt a potiori fiat denominatio.'[47] Nevertheless, they do not always apply this rule consistently. At the end of Part I, while explaining that the sins of witches exceed the sins of Adam and Eve, the text switches several times from *maleficorum* to *maleficarum*. In Part III, which deals with the practicalities of witch trials, a discussion about witnesses includes the statement 'Item sicut hereticus contra hereticum ad testificandum admittitur, ita maleficus contra maleficum.'[48] (Likewise, just as a heretic is permitted to testify against a heretic, so a [male] witch may testify against a [male] witch.)

The use of masculine references in abstract discussions of witches was probably not intended to suggest that most witches were male, especially in texts such as the *Formicarius*, *Malleus maleficarum*, and *Tableau de L'Inconstance*, which included sections explaining why women were especially attracted to witchcraft. However, it does indicate a readiness to represent witches as male without any need to justify or question such representations.

Concrete references to male witches reinforce this impression of a flexible linguistic and conceptual framework. We saw in chapter 2 that accusers and officials demonstrated no sense of cognitive dissonance when confronted with male witches. Likewise, the authors of the four treatises discussed here show no signs of confusion or need to explain the existence of male witches, despite their views that witches were predominantly female.

In the *Formicarius*, *Malleus maleficarum*, *Demonomanie*, and *Tableau de L'Inconstance*, at least one individual male witch is described at length, often recurring in the text as a kind of forensic exhibit. In the *Formicarius* and *Malleus*, this witch is Staedelin (or Stedelein), the 'grandis maleficus' of Poltingen;[49] in the *Demonomanie*, Trois-eschelles appears several times (Staedelin also makes an appearance); and de Lancre devotes several pages to a discussion of Isaac de Queyran.[50] There are many other references to male witches. Bodin, for instance, discusses various famous, learned witches, including Cornelius Agrippa, Pietro d'Abano and Guillaume de Line.[51] In the *Malleus maleficarum*, Institoris and Sprenger include a section concerning three types of witchcraft that *only* men practice.[52]

What is so striking about these passages describing male witches is that, again, the authors make no effort to justify using the terms *maleficus* or *sorcier*. Clearly, male witches were not considered by these authors to belong to a fundamentally different category of evil-doer from female witches; regardless of sex, they were all witches first and foremost.

Images

Images of witches provide additional evidence for the capacity of early modern Europeans to conceive of male witches. Demonological treatises were rarely illustrated,[53] but some of those that were offer further proof that witches were not believed to be exclusively or necessarily female. Most early modern images of witches, for instance the famous drawings and paintings of Albrecht Dürer and Hans Baldung Grien, depict female witches. There are, however, a number of images from demonological tracts that depict male witches.

The first examples are contained in Ulrich Molitor's *De laniis et phitonicis mulieribus*, which was first published at Constance in 1488.[54] Although the work's title refers specifically to women, two of the six woodcut illustrations are of male witches. In the first such illustration, three witches are flying on a forked stick while simultaneously transforming into animals. It is clear from the clothing that at least one of the figures is male (see figure 6).[55] The second of these woodcuts depicts a man riding what appears to be a wolf (see figure 7). Charles Zika has found that in this particular illustration, the witch is a man in all but one of the almost twenty versions published in the 1490s (the female version appears in the Ulm 1490–91 edition of *De laniis*).[56] Olaus Magnus' *Historia de gentibus septentrionalibus*

6 Witches in the form of animals, riding a stick.

7 Male witch riding a wolf.

8 Male and female witches; male witch gives a piece of his clothing to a devil as
a sign of homage.

(Rome, 1555) also contains illustrations of both male and female
witches. In one woodcut, a male witch is using a knotted rope to influence the winds.[57]

Finally, Francesco Maria Guazzo's *Compendium maleficarum*, first
published at Milan in 1608, is a veritable treasure trove of images of male
witches. The work contains a large number of woodcut illustrations,
almost all of which depict both men and women. One group of four
woodcuts shows men and women trampling the cross, being baptised
by the Devil, giving him clothing, and swearing allegiance to him while
standing in a magic circle (see figures 4, 3, 8 and 5 respectively). There
is no doubt that these people are witches. In all four images, a well-
dressed man is foregrounded, an equally well-dressed woman stands
immediately behind him, and a mixed group occupies the background.[58] Another illustration depicts a man and a women together

9 Male and female witches subjecting the bodies of dead infants to roasting or
boiling as a preliminary to using their fat or ashes to make noxious charms,
potions and ointments.

roasting an infant while a couple in the background prepares to boil a
child in a cauldron (see figure 9).[59]

To Charles Zika, the *De laniis* woodcut of the male witch riding
a wolf suggests that 'the gender link in representations of witchcraft
has clearly not yet been established in the 1490s'.[60] Given that this
image was reproduced in sixteenth-century editions, and that the six-
teenth- and seventeenth-century works by Olaus Magnus and Guazzo
also included depictions of male witches, we ought to push Zika's
insight farther. The (female) gender link in visual representations of
witchcraft was strong in the early modern period, as evidenced by the
fact that the majority of images depicted witches as women; however,
this link could not have been absolute. If early modern artists and printers had been incapable of imagining male witches, it is improbable that

they would have chosen to depict them, especially in illustrations of demonological tracts that furnished many descriptions of the activities of female witches.

Conclusions

Conventional assessments of demonological concepts of witchcraft and gender need revision. First, Stuart Clark's statement that demonological theory about gender and witchcraft did not conform to the patterns of prosecution appears somewhat too broad. One could argue that although patterns of language usage do not conform precisely to patterns of prosecution, they do reflect them, in that both generally include a minority and, at times, a majority, of men. There is, thus, no wide gap between demonological theory and actual prosecutions.

Second, views of early modern demonology as sex-specific, exemplified by Sigrid Brauner's assertion that 'by 1500, the sex-specificity of witches was so widely accepted that it was implicitly assumed in texts about witches'[61] and Stuart Clark's remark that it was literally unthinkable that witches should be male, are clearly overdrawn. Witchcraft theorists may have taken it for granted that witches were mostly female, but they did not treat witchcraft as sex-specific. One can interpret early modern witchcraft theory as sex-specific only by ignoring a considerable body of evidence to the contrary.

Notes

1 Trevor-Roper, *The European Witch-Craze*, 78–79.
2 E.g. Sophie Houdard, *Les Sciences du diable: Quatre Discours sur la sorcellerie, Xve–XVIIe siècle* (Paris: Editions du Cerf, 1992); Clark, *Thinking With Demons*; Ian Bostridge, *Witchcraft and its Transformations*; Jonathan Pearl, *The Crime of Crimes: Demonology and Politics in France 1520–1620* (Waterloo, Ont.: Wilfrid Laurier University Press, 1999).
3 E.g. Sydney Anglo, ed., *The Damned Art: Essays in the Literature of Witchcraft* (London: Routledge & Kegan Paul, 1977); Peter Segl, ed., *Der Hexenhammer*; Eliane Camerlynck, 'Fémininité et sorcellerie chez les

théoriciens de la démonologie à la fin du Moyen Age: Étude du *Malleus maleficarum*', *Renaissance and Reformation* 19 (1983): 13–25.

4 Christopher Baxter, 'Johann Weyer's *De Praestigiis Daemonum*: Unsystematic psychopathology', *The Damned Art*, 53–75: 53.

5 *Ibid.*, 71.

6 This debate incorporates broader issues concerning the definition and division of elite and popular culture, 'top-down' dynamics, acculturation, persecution, and state-building. For an overview see again Briggs, '"Many reasons why"'. See also Norman Cohn, *Europe's Inner Demons: The Demonization of Christians in Medieval Christendom*, rev. edn. (London: Pimlico, 1993 [Chatto & Heinemann 1975]); Larner, *Enemies of God*; Carlo Ginzburg, 'Deciphering the Sabbath', *Centres and Peripheries*, 121–138; Muchembled, 'Satanic myths and cultural reality'.

7 Heinrich Institoris and Jacob Sprenger, *Malleus maleficarum*, Speyer: Drach, 1487, fac. edn., André Schnyder, ed. (Göppingen: Kümmerle, 1991), I.6, 44. This edition is cited hereafter as Schnyder.

8 Montague Summers, trans., *The Malleus Maleficarum of Heinrich Kramer and James Sprenger* (New York: Dover, 1971 [London: John Rodker, 1928; repr. 1948]), 46.

9 Barstow, *Witchcraze*, 173.

10 Karlsen, *The Devil in the Shape of a Woman*, 3. Karlsen seems to be referring to New England authors, but she does not specify which ones or cite textual examples.

11 Susanna Burghartz, 'The equation of women and witches: A case study of witchcraft trials in Lucerne and Lausanne in the fifteenth and sixteenth centuries', *The German Underworld: Deviants and Outcasts in German History*, ed. Richard J. Evans (London and New York: Routledge, 1988), 57–74: 60.

12 *Ibid.*, 59. Burghartz cites Richard Kieckhefer, *European Witch Trials: Their Foundations in Popular and Learned Culture* (Berkeley: University of California, 1976).

13 Clark, *Thinking With Demons*, 133. Original italics.

14 *Ibid.*, 129–130.

15 Eric Wilson, 'The text and content of the *Malleus Maleficarum* (1487)', unpublished dissertation (Cambridge University, 1991), 7.

16 *Ibid.*, 11.

17 *Ibid.*, 264.

18 In his discussion of ritual inversion, Clark acknowledges that 'no language-game escapes a degree of incoherence', and that early modern beliefs about witchcraft contained 'ambivalences and contradictions'. However, he

suggests that 'these ambivalences and contradictions ought not to be over-dramatized or over-interpreted' (*Thinking with Demons*, 29–30). In the case of gender and witchcraft, ambivalences and contradictions have not been interpreted at all, or, in Clark's case, even mentioned.

19 Researchers working with English-language editions might be forgiven for failing to notice the use of masculine terminology. As discussed in the Introduction, English does not have adequate parallel terms for male and female witches, which causes some translation difficulties. In addition, the only current English translation of the *Malleus maleficarum*, the most widely cited demonological treatise, is seriously flawed. Montague Summers not only believed in witches but also approved of the *Malleus'* misogynistic passages: 'exaggerated as these may be, I am not altogether certain that they will not prove a wholesome and needful antidote in this feministic age', xxxix. More importantly, Summers rarely indicates in his translation where Institoris and Sprenger use a masculine term, and in fact distorts at least one passage by changing an original masculine term to a feminine one: in I.14, 'Dicuntur enim malefici' (Schnyder, 72) becomes 'For they are called witches (*maleficae*)' (Summers, 75). Readers will soon have a reconstituted text, a meticulous English translation and copious scholarly notes available to them in the form of Christopher S. Mackay's forthcoming publication of the *Malleus maleficarum* (Cambridge: Cambridge University Press).

20 Brauner, *Fearless Wives*, 123.

21 Schnyder, 11.

22 Adrian Johns, 'Introduction: The book of nature and the nature of the book', *The Nature of the Book: Print and Knowledge in the Making* (Chicago: Chicago University Press, 1998), 1–57.

23 *Ibid.*, 22–23.

24 Köln, 1480 and Lyons, 1669. See below.

25 Speyer, 1487 (Schnyder fac., Houghton Library Inc. 2367.5, British Library IB 8581); Lyons, 1669 (Bruce Peel Special Collections, University of Alberta, BF 1569 I59 I669; BL 719.1.18); Cologne 1494 (Houghton Library Inc. 1462); Nuremberg 1494 (Houghton Library Inc. 2090 (16.3)); Frankfurt 1588 (Houghton Library Inc. 24244. 3.305); additional editions BL 1606/312, 719.b.2, 719.b.1, 718.c.48, 232A37, IA 8634, IB 8615, IA 7503, 719.b.5, 719.b.3, IA 7468, IB 1953, 1606/345.

26 Johannes Nyder, *Formicarius*, Köln 1480, fac. edn. (Graz: Akademische Druck-und Verlagsanstalt, 1971), introd. Hans Biedermann. 5.1, 190. Italics added.

27 Ioannis Nider, *Formicarius Malleus maleficarum* vol. I (Lyons: Bourgeat 1669), 305–354: 305. Italics added.

28 Schnyder, 7. Italics added.

29 E.g. Lyons, 1669 (British Library 719.1.18): 'asserere'; Cologne, 1511 (British Library 719.b.1): 'offendere'.

30 E.g. Klaits, *Servants of Satan*, 44: 'the *Malleus* seemed to benefit from papal sanctions, as each edition reprinted Innocent's bull as a preface to the work.' The Speyer 1487 edition owned by Harvard's Houghton Library does not include the bull.

31 Lyons, 1669, 314; Köln, 1480, 201.

32 Johannes Nyder, *Formicarius*, Köln 1480. The *Formicarius* was composed *circa* 1435 but not published until 1480. Book 5, which deals with witchcraft, was often printed with the *Malleus maleficarum* and other tracts during the sixteenth and seventeenth centuries. It is sometimes cited as the *Formicarium*, and Nyder is ordinarily spelled Nider. See Hans Biedermann's introduction to the facsimile edition.

33 Heinrich Institoris and Jacob Sprenger, *Malleus maleficarum*, Speyer 1487.

34 Ulrich Molitor, *De laniis et phitonicis mulieribus*, Cologne 1489, fac. edn. (Paris: Emile Nourry, 1926). First edition Constance 1488. Facsimile includes a French translation.

35 Jean Bodin, *De la demonomanie des sorciers*, Paris 1580, facs. edn. (Hildesheim: Georg Olms, 1988). First edition.

36 Nicolaus Jacquier, Flagellum haereticorum fascinariorum, Frankfurt/Main 1581. Houghton Library 24244.172. Bound with several other tracts, including Erastus's *De lamiis* and Daneau's *De veneficis. Flagellum haereticorum fascinariorum* pp. 1–183 of volume. The *Flagellum* is a fifteenth-century tract (1458?).

37 Lambertus Danaeus [Daneau], *De veneficis*, Frankfurt/Main 1581. Houghton Library 24244.172. Bound with several other tracts (see previous note). *De veneficis* pp. 184–299 of volume. First published in 1574.

38 Petrus Binsfeld, *Tractatus de confessionibus maleficorum et sagarum recognitus & auctus*, Trier 1591. Houghton Library 24244.48. First published at Trier in 1589.

39 Nicolaus Remigius, *Daemonolatreiae Libri Tres*, Lyons 1595. Houghton Library 24244.5. First edition.

40 Pierre de Lancre, *Tableau de L'Inconstance des Mauvais Anges*, Paris 1613, abridged repr, ed. Nicole Jacques-Chaquin (Paris: Aubier, 1982). First published at Paris in 1612.

41 Friedrich Spee, *Cautio criminalis*, Frankfurt, 1632, repr., ed. Theo G.M. Van Oorschot (Tübingen and Basel: A. Franck, 1992). First published at Rinteln in 1631.

42 Nyder, 5.1, 191.

43 Schnyder, I.2, 13.

44 Nyder, 5.3, 202.

45 Bodin, 1.1, 1. Bodin is not one-hundred per cent consistent: in Bk. 4, ch. 4, he makes an abstract reference in the feminine. 'Si donc Sorciere a esté condamnee comme Sorciere, elle sera tousiours reputee Sorciere, & par consequent presumee coupable de toutes les impietés, dont les Sorciers sont notés.' (If, therefore, a witch has been condemned as a witch, she will always be reputed to be a witch, and in consequence presumed guilty of all the impieties for which witches are notorious.) Accents lacking in the original; p. 189.

46 de Lancre, 1.1, 60.

47 Schnyder, I.6, 45. We believe that the feminine usage espoused by Institoris and Sprenger was not meant to be exclusive, counter-intuitive though this seems. First, they never argue that all witches are women, merely that most of them are; second, there are instances in the text where they refer to *maleficae* but then use a masculine pronoun in the same sentence. E.g. 'Patet quod modica sit comparatio per respectum ad maleficas et eorum opera.' The final phrase 'witches and their works' uses the feminine '*maleficas*', but the pronoun 'their' is in the masculine. I.16, 79.

48 Schndyer, III.4, 198.

49 Staedelin is described at some length. One important element is his confession to having magically induced several miscarriages; this suggests, again, that male witches were not necessarily thought to practise gender-specific magic, the archer-witches of the Malleus notwithstanding. Nyder, 5.3, 202: 'stedelein grandis maleficus ... fatebatur se in certa domo vbi vir & vxor simul manebant per sua maleficia successiue in vtero vxoris prefate septem circiter infantes occidisse ita vt semper aborsum faceret in femina annis multis.' (Stedelein was a great witch ... he confessed to having killed, by his evil magic, in a certain house where a man and a woman lived together, around seven infants, one after the other, in the woman's womb, and in such a way that the woman would always abort for many years thereafter.)

50 Both Trois-eschelles and Isaac de Queyran confess to having attended witches' Sabbaths and to worshipping the Devil. Bodin, 3.5, 151; de Lancre, 2.4, 158–166.

51 Bodin, Preface.

52 Schnyder II. 16. The most important of these is archery-witchcraft. Archer-witches, or *sagitarii malefici*, have extraordinary powers of archery, which they receive from the Devil.

53 Jane P. Davidson, 'Great black goats and evil little women: The image of the witch in sixteenth-century German art', *Journal of the Rocky Mountain Medieval and Renaissance Association* 6 (1985): 141–157: 143.

54 *Ibid.* Charles Zika suggests that *De laniis* was first published in 1489.

55 We concur with Zika's interpretation of this image. Zika, 'Dürer's witch, riding women and moral order', *Dürer and his Culture*, eds. Dagmar Eichberger and Charles Zika (Cambridge: Cambridge University Press, 1998), 118–140: 132.

56 *Ibid.*

57 Davidson, 'Great black goats', 151.

58 Francesco Maria Guazzo, *Compendium maleficarum* [Milan 1608], ed. Montague Summers, trans. E.A. Ashwin (New York: Dover, 1988 [London: John Rodker, 1929]), bk. I, ch. VI, pp. 14–15.

59 *Ibid.*, bk. II, ch. II, p. 89.

60 Zika, 'Dürer's witch', 133.

61 Brauner, *Fearless Wives*, 13.

CONCEPTUAL WEBS:
THE GENDERING OF WITCHCRAFT

So far, we have concentrated on constructing the male witch as a valid historical subject. In this final chapter, we wish to change gear and attempt to answer the question of how early modern Europeans, specifically witchcraft theorists, made sense of male witches. Given that they generally associated witchcraft more strongly with women than with men, it seems at first rather odd that early modern authors did not address explicitly the (to us) apparent anomaly of the male witch. However, as we have suggested so far, the nonchalance with which early modern Europeans approached the concept of the male witch suggests his existence was taken for granted. Although it is somewhat problematic to approach the question this way, asking why early modern witchcraft theorists did not regard male witches as anomalous – in other words, why there was no conceptual barrier to them – provides a useful starting point for developing an integrative interpretation of the gendering of witchcraft.

In this chapter, we argue, first, that early modern theorists were unperturbed by male witches because they were already familiar with them in the guise of ancient and medieval heretics and sorcerers. Our second, more speculative, argument concerns the feminisation of the witch. The most essential feature of the early modern witch (as understood under the 'elaborated concept' of witchcraft) was her or his subservient relationship with the Devil, who duped men and especially women into worshipping him. The witch was thus by definition weak-minded, a trait that had been associated from antiquity with women. A man accused of being a witch was also, therefore, implicitly feminised. In one sense, this feminisation lends support to Stuart Clark's argument for a binary structure underlying the gendering of witchcraft; on the other hand, it cautions us against allowing that binary structure to become too rigid to accommodate flexible gender constructions.[1]

Ancient and medieval antecedents

What did medieval and early modern Europeans think about witches? There was a vast array of ideas, many of them indeed drawn from pre-Christian sources. Their origins can be suspected in ancient magic, love-spells, and the cults of various gods and goddesses; in the religious and magical practices of pre-Christian Europeans of the most varied ethnicities (Celts, Teutons, Slavs, Basques, Etruscans, Latins, Greeks, etc.); in European folklore, perhaps also dating from pre-Christian times, about spirits, fairies, goblins, demons, banshees, imps, elves, kobolds, and spirits in animal form; in shamanistic ideas and practices such as those of the *benandanti*,[2] which seem to arise from the deep past of some common or widely diffused Eurasian heritage; in particular Scriptural passages that *seem* to refer to what Europeans think of and we refer to in English as witches or sorcerers ('Thou shalt not suffer a witch to live',[3] Exodus 22, 17–18).

Edward Peters has argued that the classic early modern witch 'was a distinct type' that should not be confused with earlier types of magic-user.[4] However, historians of witchcraft and witch-beliefs, including Peters, agree generally that the night-flying witch who made a pact with the Devil and worshipped him in exchange for supernatural powers was a learned, cumulative construct that developed over centuries of Christian demonisation of heretics and sorcerers. If we trace these two elements in the witch's heritage, we see that early modern authors would have been thoroughly familiar with the idea that both men and women could be Devil-worshippers and magicians. There was, therefore, no reason for witchcraft theorists to be surprised or confused by the existence of male witches.

One of the central aspects of learned early modern witch-belief was the witches' Sabbath, where witches gathered to worship the Devil, dance, feast, indulge in sexual orgies, and practise cannibalism and infanticide (see figure 10). The Sabbath myth and its components have occupied the attention of many scholars, who have attempted to demonstrate, variously, either elite or folk origins.[5] The debate over origins need not concern us here; what is important, for the present purpose, is that learned ideas about the witches' Sabbath correspond very closely to traditional stereotypes concerning heretics.

Norman Cohn has argued that the early modern notion of the Sabbath evolved from much older fantasies about various dissenting groups. Early Christian apologists encountered widespread beliefs that

10 Male and female witches dining at the witches' Sabbath.

Christians engaged in cannibalism, infanticide and incest;[6] Jews were ridiculed in the ancient world for supposedly worshipping a donkey-god;[7] and the Catiline conspirators were believed by Dio Cassius to have practised ritual murder.[8] Christianity survived such accusations, of course, but over the centuries,

> tales of erotic debauches, infanticide and cannibalism were revived and applied to various religious outgroups in medieval Christendom. In the process they were integrated more and more firmly into the corpus of Christian demonology. ... the powers of darkness loomed larger and larger in these tales, until they came to occupy the very centre of the stage. Erotic debauches, infanticide and cannibalism gradually took on a new meaning, as so many manifestations of a religious cult of Satan, so many expressions of Devil-worship.[9]

Montanists, Paulicians, Bogomils, Waldensians, Cathars, and other groups were all believed by Catholic authorities to engage in these practices.[10]

When early modern authors described the activities of witches, they incorporated these stereotypical charges against heretics. Johannes Nider, for instance, explained that in Lausanne certain witches cooked and ate infants,[11] and Guazzo wrote that at their gatherings witches 'sing in honour of the Devil the most obscene songs ... and then in the foulest manner they copulate with their demon lovers.'[12] Given that so many of the early witchcraft theorists were inquisitors (Jacquier, Nider, Institoris, and Nicolas Eymeric, to name a few), their incorporation of these elements is not surprising. Inquisitors would, presumably, have been familiar with these alleged activities of heretics, and, since witches were Devil-worshippers, it makes sense that they would believe them to engage in similar practices.

The important thing about the similarity between witches and heretics is that, as William Monter has pointed out, 'heresy itself was not sex-linked'.[13] Both men and women participated in heretical movements, and both men and women were thought to participate in the traditional depravities. Therefore, theorists who believed that witches practised similar evil acts would have had no reason for surprise at the notion that men took part, despite their view that women were especially susceptible. In short, there were precedents for the participation of men in Devil-worship.

Monter made a similar connection in his 1976 study of the Jura region in the fifteenth century, where the authorities in three dioceses – Geneva, Lausanne and Sion – prosecuted more male than female witches. Monter found that these exceptions 'to the fifteenth-century trend to equate witchcraft with women' were also those dioceses 'which first popularly identified sorcery with heresy', specifically, with Waldensianism. He suggests that because heresy was not sex-linked, 'in a region where heresy and witchcraft were closely connected in the popular mind, witchcraft was not originally sex-linked either.'[14] The corollary of Monter's argument is that in regions where heresy and witchcraft were *not* closely connected, witchcraft was sex-linked.[15] Although we have reservations about Monter's causal correlations, his evidence suggests that a conceptual link between witches and heretics could have kept the door open, as it were, for male witches.

Early modern witchcraft theorists incorporated stereotypes about heretics into their beliefs about witches, but they rarely discussed particular heretics as simple heretics (that is, without the suggestion that they were also sorcerers). Demonological texts are chock-full of references to famous magic-users from classical, biblical, and secular sources. Such references were usually included to support the authors' views concerning witches' powers. For instance, when Institoris and Sprenger argue that witches have the power to transform men into animals, they cite the example of Circe, the sorceress who transformed Odysseus' companions into swine.[16] Many of these references describe male magic-users, who seem to have been in abundant supply in the ancient and medieval world. These figures, more so than medieval heretics, provided precedents that prevented witchcraft theorists from developing a conceptual barrier to the idea of male witches. In addition, the consistent presence of male magic-users over such a long period indicates a wider degree of acceptance of the notion that access to magical power was not limited to women.

The evidence of Greek and Latin curse tablets indicates that the practice of magic was widespread and that men participated in it in large numbers. In a recent essay, Daniel Ogden states that over 1,600 curse tablets, or *defixiones*, are currently known to scholars.[17] These tablets, which were usually made of lead, bore written curses of various kinds, regarding litigation, politics, competition, trade, erotic matters, and prayers for justice.[18] They have been found in Britain and in every country around the Mediterranean, and date from the early fifth or even sixth century BCE to the eighth century CE.[19]

Ogden suggests that 'many curse tablets were probably made, activated and deposited by amateurs on an ad hoc basis.'[20] Specialists may have assisted in the manufacturing of tablets, for instance by inscribing a curse text, but, as Ogden points out, these specialists were not necessarily magicians. On the other hand, long and complex curse texts requiring magical formulae must have depended on magical handbooks.[21] In addition, 'since obscurity and difficulty were important sources of "power" for ancient magic, it may have been more satisfying to visit a professional, one of supposedly arcane knowledge and mysterious skills, for the text of a tablet'.[22]

Whether or not the author of a curse tablet was a professional, 'the vast majority of all curse tablets, including erotic ones, [were] written by men.' Furthermore, Ogden cautions, 'it is possible that some of the curse tablets contain the actual words of women, but we must remember that they are largely formulaic, and we can never be sure that even an apparently personally worded text was not composed with the aid of or simply by a male (professional or otherwise).'[23] Although this evidence does not necessarily show that men were more active participants in magic than women, it indicates clearly that men were 'everyday' magic-users. Similarly, the sexual spells contained in a collection of early Christian

Coptic texts suggest that men used magic; several of the spells are designed to cause a woman to love a man, and one is an erotic spell for a man to obtain a male lover.[24]

As both Daniel Ogden and Fritz Graf have pointed out, the evidence of curse tablets and magical papyri does not match up with literary representations of magic as a female activity: 'In Theocritus as well as Virgil, or in the elegiac poets, and generally in the great majority of the literary texts, it is women who practice magic, whether erotic or of another kind. This situation amounts to an astonishing reversal of what we find in the epigraphic texts and the [magical] recipes on the papyri.'[25] We shall return to this important point later in the chapter. For now, we wish merely to note that this evidence demonstrates that the literary emphasis on female practitioners of magic does not tell the whole story about magic use in the ancient world.

Considering this overemphasis on women in ancient literary texts, which are far more likely to have been known to early modern authors than curse tablets, it is all the more striking to find Jean Bodin citing many ancient examples of *male* magic-users. In his preface to *De la demonomanie des sorciers*, Bodin lists, as *sorciers*, Orpheus, Aristeas the Proconnesian, Cleomedes the Astypalian, Hermotimus of Clazomenae, Apollonius of Tyana, and Romulus.[26] None of these ancient *sorciers* corresponds very closely to the early modern witch, but Bodin evidently believed that they were of the same breed. He mentions them in order to counter the arguments of sceptics, and refers to Orpheus as a 'maistre Sorcier'.[27]

Biblical texts, including the Acts of the Apostles, furnished additional examples of male magic-users. The female Witch of Endor was cited very frequently in demonological texts, but so were the Pharaoh's magicians and Simon Magus. Ulrich Molitor, for instance, discusses Simon Magus at some length in *De laniis*. In a section dealing with whether *malefici* and *strigae* could transform men into animals with the aid of the Devil, Molitor describes Simon's deception of the Emperor Nero: 'Sic symon magus perstrinxit oculos neronis & carnifices qui

decollando arietem. credidit se symonem decollasse. in oculis suis min-
isterio dyaboli perstrictis deceptus.'[28] Nero's executioners beheaded a
ram, but because Simon, with the aid of the Devil, 'bound' the
Emperor's eyes, Nero believed that Simon had been beheaded.

In addition to the various ancient literary sources at early modern
authors' disposal, medieval sources and society provided many examples of male magic-users. Valerie Flint and Richard Kieckhefer have both
argued that magic was widespread in medieval Europe, despite official
prohibitions against it. Of the early medieval period, Flint says that it 'was
remarkably well supplied with influential and respected harioli, aus-
pices, sortilegi, and incantatores';[29] in the later medieval centuries,
Kieckhefer says, 'we find various types of people involved in diverse magical activities.'[30] These people and their activities are described in a range
of medieval sources. For example, Isidore of Seville's *Etymologiae* provided an encyclopedic summary of magic-users and their special powers.
His work was incorporated in later tracts against magic, including those
by Rabanus Maurus and Burchard of Worms, who wrote in the ninth and
early eleventh centuries, respectively.[31]

Specific references to male magic-users are not difficult to find. In
his *The History of the Franks*, Gregory of Tours describes a man named
Desiderius, who, Gregory says, 'practised the foul arts of necromancy'.
Another man, who claimed to possess holy relics, turned out to own 'a
big bag filled with the roots of various plants; in it, too, were moles'
teeth, the bones of mice, bears' claws and bear's fat', which the Bishop
Ragnemod 'recognised ... as witchcraft'.[32] Gervais of Tilbury wrote in
his *Otia Imperialia* (*c.* 1215) about an English magician at the court of
Roger II of Sicily; this magician found the burial place of Virgil,
unearthed the poet's bones, and took his book of magic.[33]

Other male figures appear in accounts of prosecutions for magic
use. In the fourteenth and early fifteenth centuries, many of these men
were ritual magicians or necromancers. Early in the fourteenth century,
three men – Bernard Délicieux (1319) and Matteo and Galeazzo
Visconti (1320) – were tried for using necromancy against Pope John

XXII.[34] At the court of Charles VI of France, at least four men were charged with practising sorcery after claiming to be able to cure the king's illness with magic. The second of the four men, Jehan de Bar, confessed to invoking demons, engaging in Devil-worship and practising ritual magic. He was condemned and burned in 1398.[35] In 1403, two men, named Poinson and Briquet, presented themselves to the king 'with the pretense of being able to discover the cause of the king's disease'. They set themselves up in the woods outside the town gate, where they built a magical circle of iron and made 'magical invocations, which apparently produced no results whatsoever'. Both men were arrested and later burned.[36]

Books of magic, such as the Munich handbook, offer further evidence that magic was both widespread and practised by men.[37] Ritual demonic magic of the kind found in such books was a masculine preserve; more specifically, it seems to have been the specialty of a 'clerical underworld'. Richard Kieckhefer asserts that necromancy 'was not a peripheral phenomenon in late medieval society and culture', and that fears concerning such magic were 'grounded in realistic awareness that necromancy was in fact being practised, and in an almost universally shared conviction that it could work'.[38]

If this was indeed the case, then it helps explain why, despite their general understanding that women were more prone than men to witchcraft, early modern authors never claimed that witchcraft was wholly sex-specific. Witchcraft theorists and their readers, especially in the fifteenth century, were not only the heirs of a long intellectual and cultural heritage that recognised the existence of male magic-users. They were also likely to have been familiar with necromancy and to have known that its practitioners were men. It would have been difficult, to say the least, to construct the argument that men could not be witches, since evidence to the contrary was all around.

Having said that, one is forced to ask why witchcraft theorists persisted in stating that women had a greater natural propensity to witchcraft than men did. The situation in the early modern period is analogous to that of the Greek and Roman worlds; as we have seen, ancient authors represented magic as something practised by women, despite the fact that men also practised magic. Early modern authors did not, as we have argued in chapter 4, exclude male practitioners from their discussions; however, explicit statements such as Pierre de Lancre's comment that 'la femme a plus d'inclination naturelle à la sorcellerie que l'homme. C'est pourquoi il y a plus de femmes Sorcières que d'hommes' (woman has a greater natural inclination to witchcraft than man. That is why there are more female witches than male) represented witchcraft as a predominantly female activity.[39] The fact that witchcraft theorists could hold this view and, at the same time, discuss male witches in their texts, suggests that the gendering of witchcraft was a complex affair.

Gendering witchcraft

In the previous section, we attempted to demonstrate that the lack of a conceptual barrier to the idea of male witches can be explained in part by witchcraft theorists' familiarity with various ancient and medieval prototypes. In this final section, we shall address the question of what it meant, in conceptual terms, to label a man as a witch within a framework that both explicitly and implicitly feminised witchcraft.

On one level, the feminisation of witchcraft is obvious. The claims of Nider, Institoris and Sprenger, and de Lancre, among others, that witchcraft was practised mostly by women identified it clearly as a female activity. Did this mean that men who practised witchcraft were regarded as feminine? Not really – or not in any overtly *sexed* way. Male witches were not depicted explicitly as feminine; however, they were associated with certain traits that feminised them implicitly.

Fritz Graf's explanation of the 'mismatch' between ancient literary representations of magic and the reality of magical practice suggests one avenue of exploration. He argues that magic, especially erotic magic, was a 'secret weapon' in male social competition, a weapon that

---

is too
the other hand, it is
ern authors and their
that male witches were,
ionably masculine. In any
uropeans perceived the body
. According to Lyndal Roper,

ody is one of its most fundamental
heories of the body, whether explicit
a sharp division between the body and
ay articulate a profound interconnection
ntal, physical and spiritual. Among the issues
und concepts of the body are questions of indi-
w we define the boundaries of a person and his or
with other people, living or dead; the causal links
illness or other kinds of physical harm and psychic, emo-
or spiritual powers; and the nature of what we might call a
rson' and his or her relation with the divine.[55]

he body of the witch, a person who crosses many boundaries, including that between the physical and spiritual realms, is a critical site for examining early modern culture. There are some studies that deal with the body of the witch, but they focus on female witches only.[56] A serious study of the early modern perceptions of the body of the male witch would add to our understanding not only of witch-beliefs, but also of the ways in which the relationships described by Lyndal Roper were constructed.[57]

was 'unworthy of the ideal warrior of the world of men'.[40]
used magic stepped 'over the borderlines of male behavic
'a true man does not need … magic – the only male sorcere
funny foreign specialists.'[41] If we adopt Graf's interpretati
men's attitudes toward male magic use, we can read early
ments about the predominance of female witches as imp
to male readers that practising magic was womanish b
is an intriguing line of thought, and suggests a depth
witches that goes beyond what other scholars have ha
subject. Early modern anxieties concerning (female)
to interfere with men's minds and bodies, and esp
procreative abilities, have been addressed by variou.
idea that authors of demonological treatises may h
level, trying to dissuade men in particular from be
not been explored.

Unfortunately, early modern authors do not c
make convenient statements about 'real' men nc
They do not even attempt to portray male witch
obvious sense. The male witches described in c
not homosexual;[42] indeed, even their demon lc
are not described as wearing women's clothi.
occupations, or having feminine habits. So
witches were feminised looks like a red herrin.
only if one seeks nothing but examples of overt....
spond to modern views on masculinity and femininity. When
broaden our perspective to accommodate earlier concepts and less overt
means of feminising men, we find several clues.

For instance, there are tantalising hints that some male witches may
have had certain physical attributes associated with women. In her book
The Color of Angels: Cosmology, Gender and the Aesthetic Imagination,
Constance Classen explores the embodiment of gender codes and hier-
archies through the senses.[44] According to Classen, 'along with being
assigned different sensory qualities', such as 'hot' or 'cold', 'men and

Peter wished his servants to arrest the aforementioned Staedelin, their
limbs and bodies were seized by such trembling, and their nostri
assailed by such a great stench, that they doubted whether they w
dare to grab the witch.)[53]

Admittedly, these are only two instances of male witche
ing what Bodin and Nider may or may not have thought r
attributes.[54] As evidence of the gendering of witcho
scanty to permit one to draw solid conclusions. On
not entirely implausible, in our view, that early mo
readers may have regarded such traits as signs
if not overtly feminine, at least not unques
case, the question of how early modern
of the male witch ought to be explore

How a culture imagines the
and revealing elements …
or implicit, may assume
the mind, or they
between what is n
which cluster a
viduation, h
her bond
between

'grandis malefic...
immortalised by Johannes Nid...
Nider tells the reader that when Staedelin w...
great stench: 'cum sepe dictus iudex petrus antefatum
[Staedelin] capere vellet per suos famulos tantus tremor manibus eorum
incussus est & corporibus & naribus illapsus tam malus fetor vt se fere
desperarent an maleficum inuadere auderent.' (When the said judge

There is one element of the gendering of witchcraft that may be tackled with more confidence. When explaining the reasons for women's greater susceptibility to becoming witches, both sceptics[58] and believers in witchcraft attributed it first and foremost to women's intellectual fragility. The misogyny of learned witch-beliefs has been much reviewed by scholars, and there is no need to cover the same ground again here, except to recall Stuart Clark's remarks that 'the association of witchcraft with women was ... built on entirely unoriginal foundations': Aristotelian physiology, a 'deeply entrenched Christian hostility to women as the originators of sin', and many commentaries by the Church fathers and medieval writers on the faults and vices of women.[59] Clark also points out that 'the experts on witchcraft ... were entirely representative of their age and culture' in terms of their views about women, and that 'they showed little interest in exploring the gender basis of witchcraft or in using it to denigrate women.'[60]

There are several valuable studies of demonological views of women, including Clark's own elegant and illuminating analysis of the binary structure underlying such ideas (see chapter 1).[61] However, this subset of witchcraft historiography lacks an exploration of the conceptual relationship between male witches and the association of women with witchcraft. We have already touched on perceptions of the body. We shall now turn to the connection between witchcraft and weak-mindedness. The starting point for this investigation is the learned view of women's susceptibility to witchcraft. Discussions of why most witches were women are not only expressions of learned misogyny; they are also definitions of the most essential characteristic of the early modern witch.

In the *Malleus maleficarum*, Institoris and Sprenger furnish a detailed explanation for the predominance of female witches.[62] This discussion hinges on their association of women with mental weakness; over and over again, they explain the greater number of female witches in terms of the intellectual feebleness of women. To begin with, women are more credulous than men, which is why the Devil, whose chief aim

is to corrupt faith, prefers to approach them instead of men.[63] Institoris
and Sprenger elaborate on this point by drawing on various authorities
to demonstrate that women are impressionable,[64] intellectually child-
like,[65] quick to abjure their faith,[66] excessively emotional,[67] have weak
memories, and lack discipline.[68] The statement that 'all witchcraft
comes from carnal lust, which is in women insatiable'[69] is notorious;
however, the key to Institoris and Sprenger's view of women's susceptibility to witchcraft is reflected more accurately in the following remark:
'quod in omnibus viribus tam anime quam corporis cum sint defectu-
ose non mirum si plura maleficia in eos quos emulantur fieri procurant.'
(Because they are defective in all essences, as much of the mind as of the
body, it is no wonder if they endeavour to cause more misfortunes in
those whom they envy.)[70] Their insatiable carnal lust derives from
women's fundamental weaknesses, which also form the basis of witchcraft. If women were not so weak, they would not be such inviting targets for the Devil's temptations, nor would they fall prey to them and
abjure their faith, which, the authors of the *Malleus* say, 'est fundamen-
tum in maleficis'.[71]

At no point do Institoris and Sprenger say that all witches are
women, or suggest that abjuration of faith is not common to all witches,
whether male or female. We can infer from their arguments that the
explanation concerning female witches is based not only on traditional
stereotypes of women, but also on a prior conceptual link between
weakness, particularly intellectual weakness, and witchcraft. This link
constitutes the heart of the early modern concept of the witch and of the
feminisation of witchcraft. According to the logic of Christian perceptions of magic as demonic (the 'elaborated concept'), witches were necessarily weak-minded, because they sought out the Devil, or were
tricked or seduced by him, and willingly became his servants. Both men
and women could be intellectually weak, and therefore both could be
ensnared by the Devil; however, because this sort of weakness had been
regarded since antiquity as a particularly feminine failing, witchcraft was
inevitably feminised.[72]

In later antiquity, early Christians, confronted not only by the 'omnipresence' of magic in the pagan world,[73] but also with accusations that they themselves practised magic, fought back. They identified the pagan deities and *daimones* as the evil demons of the Bible, and characterised magic, which involved invoking the gods and *daimones*, as the worship of demons. Valerie Flint summarises the process as follows:

> The characterisation of 'magic' as the work solely of wicked demons, and of 'sorcerers' and 'magicians' as their servants, stemmed from two convergent developments. In the first place, the concept of the 'daimon' changed ... In the second, 'magia', or 'magic', became the *chief* term whereby the most powerful of the emerging religions described, and condemned, the supernatural exercises of their enemies. ... [The] 'daimon' was translated ... into the evil demon of Judaic and Christian literature – a figure who could never help or co-operate with man for his good, but was instead his most bitter foe. Thus, those humans who looked to obtain supernatural help in the older ways and through an older or different 'daimon', came to be viewed by many as terminally deluded ... Sorcerers and magicians were then 'demonised' by being declared subject only to the demonic forces of evil, and were described as offering reinforcement to the most wicked of these forces' designs [original italics].[74]

There were two major consequences of this demonisation process. First, 'early Christian writers tended to see all forms of magic, even ostensibly harmless ones, as relying on demons.'[75] This perception of magic persisted through the medieval and early modern period. Natural philosophy admitted two branches of *magia*: natural magic and demonic magic. Both were occult, because their processes were secret and hidden from human intellect, but natural magic was not the work of demons. The men known as *magi* in Renaissance circles, such as Cornelius Agrippa, Marsilio Ficino, or Pico della Mirandola, defended natural magic, which rose in prominence as a subject of natural philosophy during the sixteenth and seventeenth centuries.[76]

Demonic magic, however, did not disappear. In the *Malleus malefi-carum*, for instance, Institoris and Sprenger insisted that witches and the Devil must always work in conjunction.[77] Jean Bodin states in the *Demonomanie* that 'without the pact with Satan, even if a man had all the powders, symbols, and incantations, he could cause neither man nor beast to die.'[78] In addition, the defenders of natural magic were some-times condemned as witches themselves. Both Jean Bodin and Pierre de Lancre, for example, call Cornelius Agrippa a master-witch.[79] To those who believed that all magic required the assistance of demons, anyone who engaged in it, in any form, was in fact practising Devil-worship.

From a Christian perspective, the logical consequence of the asso-ciation of magic with demons and Devil-worship was that magic-users were fools. Augustine expressed an early version of this idea in The *City of God*:

> What foolishness it is, then, or, rather, madness, to submit our-selves to demons, ... when by the true religion we are set free from those vices [anger, passivity of the soul, vanity, disquietude] in respect of which we resemble them! ... What reason is there, ... apart from folly and miserable error, for you to humble yourself to worship a being whom you do not wish to resemble in your life?[80]

Close to eleven centuries later, Jean Bodin explained that 'evil spirits tricked people in ancient times, as they still do now, in two ways: one openly, with formal pacts, by which usually only the *greatest simpletons* [masculine], *and women* were snared. The other way was to deceive vir-tuous but *very foolish men* by idolatry, and under a veil of religion [ital-ics added].'[81] In his preface to *De la demonomanie des sorciers*, he counters sceptical objections to the epistemological value of witches' confessions with the statement that the witches whose testimonies are in question 'for the most part are completely ignorant people or old women'.[82] In essence, as the *Malleus maleficarum* also suggests, people become witches because of an intellectual lack or failing (as well as a moral failing).

In these two passages, Bodin makes explicit a set of conceptual connections that more often operate only implicitly within early modern demonology.[83] The first connection, witch/weakness, is a binary construct that, within the logical framework of Christian demonology, seems to have been necessary and indivisible. The second connection, femininity/weakness/masculinity, is an asymmetrical triad. Both men and women share the trait of weakness, but it is linked far more strongly with women than with men.

When these two sets come together in early modern ideas about witches, they create a web of associations in which a person thought to be a witch is necessarily also thought, on some level, to be weak-minded. When that person is a woman, the associations link up in what we might visualise as a circle: each element – witch, weakness, woman – reinforces the other, creating, in essence, a stable system. If, however, the witch is a man, the associative dynamic is somewhat different. There is nothing in the web of associations, or in the intellectual traditions and past experiences, to prevent male witches. However, because the conceptual link between women and weakness is stronger than that between men and weakness, witches are associated more strongly with femininity. As a result, a *male* witch causes conceptual 'reverberations' within the web that associate him not only with weakness, but also with femininity.[84]

Does this feminisation of witchcraft and male witches mean that Stuart Clark is correct to argue that the early modern gendering of witchcraft was based on binarism? Clearly, his view that male witches were 'literally unthinkable' within early modern demonology is incorrect. At first glance, male witches appear to flatly contradict Clark's carefully worked-out system of correspondences between witches and women; one might, therefore, be tempted to dismiss his interpretation as fatally flawed. However, there is too much evidence of binary thinking both in early modern culture generally and in demonology in particular for us to indulge in a facile rejection of Clark's thesis. Furthermore, our examination of male witches and the way they made sense to early modern witchcraft theorists offers evidence of binarism at work on an implicit level.

What it also shows, though, is that Clark's interpretative scheme is too rigid. Early modern witchcraft theorists did not construct an exclusive conceptual correspondence between witches and women; indeed, it would have made very little sense for them to do so, given their experience with actual male witches. What they did construct was a web of associations similar in some respects to Clark's binary framework, but not so rigidly polarised as to prevent 'leakage' across the gender boundary. It is important to remember that although demonology feminised male witches, it never made them *female*. To put it another way, male witches were never reconstructed in such a manner as to make them unrecognisable as males.

The feminised male witch has important implications for the way we speak of gender and its construction in early modern Europe. Andrea Cornwall and Nancy Lindisfarne have written that the portrayal of the social construction of masculinity and femininity as strictly relational rests on 'a number of questionable assumptions, among them the idea that these qualities cannot be ascribed to a single individual at the same time'. They argue that although 'an important aspect of many hegemonic discourses is their focus on an absolute, naturalised and, typically, hierarchised male/female dichotomy whereby men and women are defined in terms of the *differences* between them', it is necessary to consider not only 'the relation *between* maleness and femaleness', but also 'how hierarchical relations between men and women reproduce differences *within* those categories [original italics].'[85] The feminised male witch is an excellent example of the construction of difference *within* a gender category, and forces us to rethink the binary model of early modern gender.

The male witch also highlights the feminisation of subordinates in early modern European culture. Witches were feared for their power, but they were also understood to be subservient to the Devil in a very literal sense. Bodin once again furnishes explicit statements of this idea, describing witches as Satan's slaves.[86] However, other signs of this sub-ordinate relationship were extremely common within demonological literature: the anal kiss, signifying homage; the Devil's sexual use of female witches, often described as painful to the witch; the necroman-tic practice of making offerings to demons; the physical beatings inflicted on disobedient witches by the Devil; and finally, the funda-mental role of the witch as the Devil's instrument for spreading evil. Like mental weakness, this subordination to the Devil bears a strong con-ceptual association with femininity via powerlessness and passivity.[87]

This chapter began by posing the question of how learned early modern Europeans made sense of male witches. On one level, the answer is fairly simple: male witches existed, so authors of witchcraft treatises incorporated them in their demonologies. Such a conclusion is not very rewarding; however, probing more deeply into the conceptual associations at work in early modern demonology uncovers a complex web that reflects not only ideas about witches but also how learned European men constructed gender.

Gender and witchcraft: popular knowledge

In times and in places where the 'elaborated concept' was not the dom-inant understanding of witchcraft and magic as necessarily a result of a pact with the Devil, all manner of traditional, 'pre-demonological', perhaps even 'pre-Christian' magic seems to have been in regular use: weather magic, either to bring about rain or to avert (or cause[88]) frost or hail; healing magic; the ritual battles of the male and female *benan-danti* against the forces of evil, described by Ginzburg; spells to cure or damage livestock or crops;[89] harm to infants (frequently by women);[90] charms that produced impotence;[91] love potions;[92] curses that crippled or killed,[93] and the like. Ideas about magic and its prac-tice seem to have existed well before and continued to exist in paral-lel with the elaboration of a logical, coherent Christian theory that identified the supernatural motive force behind all attempts at

[137]

witchcraft or perceived bewitchment as the Devil – despite Jeffrey Burton Russell's argument in his book *Witchcraft in the Middle Ages*[94] that witchcraft was, throughout the Middle Ages, Devil-worship. That certain Christians nourished *fantasies* about other people – Templars, heretics, Jews – worshipping the Devil is beyond question, but as Behringer has shown, the 'elaborated concept' of witchcraft did not prevail in the vast and disjointed European market place of ideas about witchcraft until the fifteenth century. The substance and content of charges of witchcraft did not change much as the 'elaborated concept' spread; in fact, in general, the local forms of magic from the pre-'elaborated concept' or pre-demonological period were retained but reinterpreted, as in the famous example of the *benandanti*, as the result of diabolical intervention or, more properly, as delusions produced by the Devil in those who served him. The *benandanti* studied by Carlo Ginzburg were, he claims, practitioners of ancient, pre-Christian shamanism, including shamanistic out-of-body travel experiences in a trance state. Although they were able to persuade the inquisitors at the beginning of the sixteenth century that they not only battled witches (using sorghum stalks as weapons), and even managed to persuade authorities that they could detect victims of witchcraft, a hundred years later, they had been persuaded that, at least according to the inquisitors' categories, they were themselves witches.[95] This example has been used to argue that 'the persecution of witches is an effect of the acculturation of rural areas by the religious and political elite',[96] that is, of the *reinterpretation* of magical lore, such as healing knowledge and various kinds of rituals, as *diabolical*. In many cases, when ideas about what witches did and who they were encountered coherent theories of 'diabolical witchcraft', individuals and institutions both accommodated popular discourse to learned demonology and resisted or modified specific aspects of the 'elaborated concept'.

The opposite was also true. Sometimes the ideas of learned elites had to accommodate popular belief. An early example of what would later become a widespread opinion among Protestant churchmen was that of Johannes Brenz, the Reformer of the city of Schwäbisch-Hall and the leading churchman of the Duchy of Württemberg (in south-western Germany). Brenz argued, well before Johannes Weyer developed a complete theory along these lines, that 'misfortunes such as hailstorms were sent by God, while the witches were merely deluded by Satan into thinking they had caused them'.[97] This suggests that the learned elites of Reformation Germany had reason to acknowledge that those accused of witchcraft sometimes believed that they had in fact practised magic (whether with or without the help of the Devil).

The main question regarding popular ideas about witchcraft that presents itself in the context of this book is to what extent such conceptions were gendered. In *Witches and Neighbors*, Robin Briggs notes that 'early' (meaning pre-sixteenth-century) images of witchcraft activities contained not only old women ('hags'), but also 'nubile young women, men and children', and that while some confessing witches asserted that women were more numerous than men at the witches' Sabbath, 'a fair number' insisted that the sexes were equally represented, or even that there were more men,[98] suggesting that these witches were introducing witchcraft ideas that were to some extent at odds with 'orthodox' demonology regarding the greater susceptibility of women to the Devil's lures.[99] Regarding gender, Briggs states that '[a]lthough no area of magical power was totally or consistently gendered, large parts of folk medicine and love magic tended to become feminine specialities',[100] though the *benandanti* of the Friuli were certainly popular healers, and most were men. Indeed, Briggs suggests that the widespread idea, especially in the English-speaking world, that most or almost all witches were women has to do with the fact that very few men were accused or executed in England, and that the English demonologists were guilty of an extreme misogyny that has called forth an equal and opposite reaction among many scholars. This last point is worth examining; it seems to us that English demonologists were no more or less misogynistic, say, than the authors of the *Malleus maleficarum*. It is by looking beyond England and in leaving behind the dated 'sociogenesis argument' (i.e., the notion that witches were quintessentially weak/poor/old women), which Briggs has rightly critiqued, that we can begin to understand both learned and popular concepts of witchcraft and their complexly gendered nature. In certain parts of Europe, such as sixteenth-century Finland, 'the stereotype sorcerer was a man, probably due to Finnish folk traditions and the ancient Finnish religion, in which supernatural powers were not associated with women but with men.'[101] The majority of those accused of witchcraft in Iceland were men, and unlike in English, the generic term for witch in Icelandic was masculine.[102] The grammatical gender of a word cannot, on its own, have caused the preponderance of men among those accused; although for the English-speaking world, the effects of the (implicitly) gendered word 'witch' on both the popular imagination and on scholarship should not be underestimated.

The Icelandic witch trials of the seventeenth century, as in the Basque country studied by Henningsen, coincide with 'a temporary syncretism of the witch-beliefs of the common people with those of the specialized or educated classes'.[103] Briggs and others have noted that the majority of accusations were produced at the local level, and motivated by 'fear of witchcraft in the most direct sense.'[104] Here we must look not for a belief that old, strange, poor women were, somehow, a priori, witches, but for belief in witchcraft and local, temporally specific and quite dynamic and flexible ideas about who might be a witch,[105] ideas that included all manner of popular lore about medicine, healing, and especially *maleficium*, and which, by the sixteenth century at the latest, were interacting with learned demonology in unpredictable and explosive ways. It is this last point that is crucial for understanding the complex relationship between popular and learned ideas: they were not unrelated, but when they came into conjunction, and other external factors (whether inquisitorial zeal, large-scale agrarian crises, a local crop failure, or small-scale (perceived) damages in the village or countryside) provided the impetus, either cases of 'low-level' or 'endemic' persecution or episodes of intensive or even 'epidemic' witch-hunting could ensue. It is hard to say whether learned demonologists were more or less disposed than everyone else to think that witches were more likely to be women than men, since both did think this – though not exclusively. The only real answer is that it depends where, and when. The vexed question as to whether or not learned writers accommodated their universalising demonological discourses to local conditions and ideas, or were influenced by those ideas, in order to produce this 'syncretism' – or if some other, much less straightforward process of 'influence' was afoot – is the core issue here, but it falls outside the scope of the present work and remains as a fascinating agenda for further research based on specific historical situations.

Notes

1 We have borrowed this image of the procrustean binary structure from Christopher A. Faraone, *Ancient Greek Love Magic* (Cambridge and London: Harvard University Press, 1999), ix.

2 The *benandanti* of the Friuli were healers and 'shamans' who went out in dreams to fight witches, they said, and to ensure the fertility of the crops; by the seventeenth century, they were being forced to confess to diabolical witchcraft. See Ginzburg, *Night Battles*.

3 The meaning of *m'chashefa* is actually unclear; the Septuagint translates the word *m'chashefa* as 'poisoner'. In rabbinic literature, the term is glossed as to referring to magical activities that are typically female; yet the Talmud makes it clear that these people can be men or women (*Palestinian Talmud*, Sanhedrin 7:19, 25d; *Babylonian Talmud*, Sanhedrin 67a); cf. Leviticus 20, 27, which prescribes the death penalty for a man or a woman who practises divination through a ghost or a familiar spirit. See the Hertz Chumash (*The Pentateuch and Haftorahs*, ed. Rabbi J.H. Hertz. London: Soncino, 1947), commentary to Exodus 22, 17, p. 313, which amounts to a polemic against Christian scholars' attempts to pin the blame for witch persecution on Judaism and the Hebrew Scriptures. Hertz notes that the odd wording of the injunction (such commandments are usually phrased as a direct commandment to put such a person to death) led some Jewish commentators to suggest that it is a prohibition against using the services of a sorceress/diviner, and thereby allowing her to make a living. The importance of this passage to

early modern demonologists can be gauged by the reference to it in the *Daemonologie* of James I and VI as proving the existence of witchcraft: *Daemonologie, in Forme of a Dialogue* [1597], ed. G.B. Harrison (New York: Barnes & Noble, 1966), 5.

4 Peters, *The Magician, the Witch, and the Law*, 170.

5 See e.g. Cohn, *Europe's Inner Demons*; Ginzburg, *Ecstasies*; Muchembled, 'Satanic myths and cultural reality'; Robert Rowland, '"Fantasticall and Devilishe Persons": European witch-beliefs in comparative perspective', *Centres and Peripheries*, 161–190; Gustav Henningsen, '"The ladies from outside": An archaic pattern of the witches' Sabbath', *Centres and Peripheries*, 191–215; Éva Pócs, *Between the Living and the Dead: A Perspective on Witches and Seers in the Early Modern Age*, trans. Szilvia Rédey and Michael Webb (Budapest: Central European University Press, 1999). Carlo Ginzburg's ambitious attempts to locate the origins of the witches' Sabbath in a prehistoric shamanistic culture are especially fascinating but also problematic.

6 Cohn, *Europe's Inner Demons*, 1–4.

7 *Ibid.*, 5–6.

8 *Ibid.*, 6.

9 *Ibid.*, 36.

10 See *ibid.*, 35–78 for detailed discussions of the accusations against these groups. Similar stereotypes extend to the present day, with belief in covert groups that practise Devil-worship 'spread very widely through the Western world'. The alleged practices of such groups 'include human sacrifice, cannibalism and depraved sexual orgies.' Jean La Fontaine, 'The history of the idea of Satan and Satanism', *Witchcraft and Magic in Europe: The Twentieth Century*, 88–93: 87.

11 Nyder, 5.3, 202: 'in lausanensi ducatu quidam malefici proprios natos infantes coxerant & comederant'.

12 Guazzo, *Compendium maleficarum*, 38.

13 Monter, *Witchcraft in France and Switzerland*, 23.

14 *Ibid.*, 22–24. Monter bases his hypothesis of a connection between witchcraft and heresy on linguistic evidence: in Geneva, Lausanne and Sion, 'the earliest vernacular words for "witch" [e.g. *vaudois*] were distinctly derived from words for "heretic".' In other areas, where most witches were women, vernacular terms rooted in sorcery, such as *casserode* and *genauche*, were more common. pp. 22–23.

15 Monter seems to use the term 'sex-linked' only when the majority of witches are women. Witchcraft is not sex-linked, it appears, when the majority are men. This is another obvious instance of historians'

conceptual bias against the existence of male witches. There is no logical reason to view witchcraft as sex-linked in one instance and not in the other – unless, that is, one is employing asymmetrical standards of sex-relatedness.

16 Schnyder, II.1.8, 119: 'famosissima maga circes mutauerit socios ulixis in bestias'. This reference to Circe derives from Augustine, *The City of God*, 18.17 (ed. and trans. R.W. Dyson). It appears in almost identical form in many works on magic, including Isidore's *Etymologiae*, Bk. VIII, Ch. IX, *PL* 82, 310–314: 311 (ed. J.-P. Migne), and Rabanus Maurus's *De magicis artibus*, *PL* 110, 1095–1110: 1097 (ed. J.-P. Migne).

17 Daniel Ogden, 'Binding spells: Curse tablets and voodoo dolls in the Greek and Roman worlds', *Witchcraft and Magic in Europe: Ancient Greece and Rome*, eds. Bengt Ankarloo and Stuart Clark (Philadelphia: University of Pennsylvania, 1999; London: Athlone, 1999), 1–90: 1.

18 *Ibid.*, 31.

19 *Ibid.*, 4–6.

20 *Ibid.*, 54.

21 *Ibid.*, 55.

22 *Ibid.*, 57.

23 *Ibid.*, 62–63.

24 Anon., 'Sexual spells', *Ancient Christian Magic: Coptic Texts of Ritual Power*, ed. Marvin W. Meyer and Richard Smith (Princeton: Princeton University Press, 1999), 147–181.

25 Graf, *Magic in the Ancient World*, 185.

26 Bodin, Preface, *Demonomanie*, unpaginated.

27 *Ibid.*, 1.1, 3.

28 Molitor, *De laniis*, unpaginated.

29 Valerie I.J. Flint, *The Rise of Magic in Early Medieval Europe* (Princeton, NJ: Princeton University Press, 1994 [1991]), 60.

30 Richard Kieckhefer, *Magic in the Middle Ages* (Cambridge: Cambridge University Press, 1997 [1989]), 56.

31 Isidore of Seville, *Etymologiae*; Rabanus Maurus, *De magicis artibus*; Burchard of Worms, *Decretum* Bk. X (*De incantatoribus et auguribus*), *PL* 140, 831–854 (ed. J.-P. Migne).

32 Gregory of Tours, *The History of the Franks*, Bk. IX, Ch. 6, trans. Lewis Thorpe (Harmondsworth: Penguin, 1985 [1974]), 483–485.

33 Peters, *The Magician, the Witch, and the Law*, 54.

34 Richard Kieckhefer, *Forbidden Rites: A Necromancer's Manual of the Fifteenth Century*, Magic in History (University Park, PA: Pennsylvania State University Press, 1998 [Sutton, 1997]), 1.

35 Jan R. Veenstra, *Magic and Divination at the Courts of Burgundy and France: Text and Context of Laurens Pignon's* Contre les devineurs *(1411)* (Leiden: Brill, 1998), 68. The first man involved was Arnaud Guillaume, who attended the king in 1393.

36 *Ibid.*, 72–73.

37 For the Munich handbook, see Kieckhefer, *Forbidden Rites*. For other books of magic, see *Conjuring Spirits: Texts and Traditions of Medieval Ritual Magic*, ed. Claire Fanger, Magic in History (University Park, PA: Pennsylvania State University Press, 1998), especially the essay by Juris Lidaka, '*The Book of Angels, Rings, Characters and Images of the Planets*: Attributed to Osbern Bokenham', pp. 32–75.

38 Kieckhefer, *Forbidden Rites*, 10.

39 de Lancre, 1.3, 89.

40 Graf, *Magic in the Ancient World*, 186–187.

41 *Ibid.*, 189.

42 William Monter found in his study of the Jura region that many men accused of witchcraft were also accused of 'grave sexual crimes', including sodomy, but this does not necessarily mean that male witches in general were thought to engage in homosexual activity – on the contrary, it could suggest that sodomites also engaged in witchcraft. *Witchcraft in France and Switzerland*, 135–136.

43 See e.g. Bodin, *Demonomanie*, 2.7, 107. Bodin refers to Giovanni Francesco Pico, Prince of Mirandola, on the subject of two sorcerer-priests whose demon lovers were female: 'Ian François Pic Prince de la Mirande escript auoir veu vn Pretre Sorcier nommé Benòist Berne aagé de lxxx. ans, qui disoit auoir eu copulation plus de XL. ans auec vn Démon desguisé en femme ... Et si escript auoir veu encores vn autre Prestre aagé de LXX. ans, qui confessa aussi auoir eu semblable copulation plus de cinquante and auec vn Demon en guise de femme, qui fut aussi bruslé.' See Walter Stephens, *Demon Lovers: Witchcraft, Sex and the Crisis of Belief* (Chicago: Chicago University Press, 2002). This book appeared too late for us to consult it.

44 Constance Classen, 'The scented womb and the seminal eye: Embodying gender codes through the senses', *The Color of Angels: Cosmology, Gender and the Aesthetic Imagination* (London and New York: Routledge, 1998), 63–85. Classen's discussion covers a very wide range of sources from the ancient, medieval and early modern periods, and the views she describes were not necessarily constant or consistent. Nevertheless, her work on the gendering of the senses offers an intriguing way of opening up the discussion of the gendering of witchcraft. Classen herself argues that 'the

witch-hunters of the fifteenth, sixteenth, and seventeenth centuries took the traditional negative stereotypes of women's sensory traits and practices and made of them a diabolic female sensorium in which each of the senses was dedicated to evil', 78–79. This interesting interpretation is, unfortunately, marred by Classen's conclusion that 'the witch-hunts were, at least in part, designed to put the fear of God and of the executioner into women, and to clamp down on attempts by women either to aspire to male forms of power, or to empower themselves through traditional women's work', 82.

45 *Ibid.*, 63–65. Merry Wiesner's *Women and Gender in Early Modern Europe* provides a general overview of attitudes toward women's bodies. On the association of women with the physical, see also Caroline Walker Bynum, 'Women mystics and eucharistic devotion in the thirteenth century', *Fragmentation and Redemption: Essays on Gender and the Human Body in Medieval Religion* (New York: Zone, 1992), 119–150: 146–150. On early modern theologies of the body, see Roper, 'Exorcism and the theology of the body', *Oedipus and the Devil*, 171–198. On sexual difference and gender construction more generally, see Joan Cadden, *Meanings of Sex Difference in the Middle Ages: Medicine, Science, and Culture* (Cambridge: Cambridge University, 1995 [1993]), 167–227; and Thomas Laqueur, *Making Sex: Body and Gender from the Greeks to Freud* (Cambridge, MA: Harvard University Press, 1990).

46 Classen, *The Color of Angels*, 66.

47 *Ibid.*, 70.

48 *Ibid.*, 71.

49 Bodin, *Demonomanie*, 2.1, 52. The date given on this page is 1574 (see note 52), but this is surely an error for 1571.

50 *Ibid.*, 3.3, 134. 'Et me souuient que Trois-eschelles Manseau estant en la presence d'vn Roy, fist vn traict de son mestier, qui estonna le Roy à vray dire … le Roy le fist sortir, & ne le voulut on ques voir, tellement que au lieu d'estre fauory, on luy fist son procés, & fut condamné comme Sorcier …' (I recall that Trois-eschelles, while in the presence of the king, performed a trick of his craft, which amazed the king, truth to tell … the king sent him out and desired never to see him again, so much so that instead of being favoured, he was tried and condemned as a witch …)

51 *Ibid.*, 2.4, 80. 'Et n'y a pas long temps, c'est à dire lan M.D. LXXI. entre ceux qui furent deferez Sorciers par l'aueugle, qui fut pendu à Paris … ' (Not long ago, that is, in the year 1571, among those who had been denounced as witches by the blind one, who was hanged at Paris …)

52 *Ibid.*, 2.1, 52. 'Et mesme l'aueugle Sorcier, qui fut pendu à Paris l'an M.D. LXXIIII, & qui en accusa cent cinquante, & plus …' (Even the blind witch

who was hanged at Paris in 1574, and who denounced one hundred and
   fifty others, or even more …)
53 Nyder, 5.4, 202.
54 Bodin does state that witches are foul-smelling, but he explains that this is
   because they copulate with demons, who may take on the bodies of the
   dead. Women have sweeter breath than men, but their intimacy with Satan
   causes them to become unnaturally hideous and foul. 3.3, 133: 'les anciens
   ont appellé les Sorcieres *foetentes* … pour la puanteur d'icelles, qui vient
   comme ie croy de la copulation des Diables, lesquels peut estre prennent
   des corps des pendus, ou autres semblables pour les actions charnelles et
   corporelles'.
55 Roper, 'Exorcism and the theology of the body', 171.
56 See e.g. Roper, 'Exorcism and the theology of the body', and 'Witchcraft
   and fantasy'; Purkiss, *The Witch in History*; Barstow, *Witchcraze*; Classen,
   The Color of Angels.
57 Another important avenue of inquiry is 'the body as object and target of
   power', suggested by Michel Foucault. *Discipline and Punish: The Birth
   of the Prison*, trans. Alan Sheridan (New York: Vintage, 1995; orig.
   Surveiller et punir. Naissance de la prison, Paris: Gallimard, 1976), 136.
   Roper engages to some degree with this issue in the two essays cited above.
58 For example, Johann Weyer, who published his attack on witch-hunting,
   De praestigiis daemonum, in 1563, wrote that 'most often … the Devil
   thus influences the female sex, that sex which by reason of temperament
   is inconstant, credulous, wicked, uncontrolled in spirit, and (because of its
   feelings and affections, which it governs only with difficulty) melancholic;
   he especially seduces stupid, worn out, unstable old women.' *De praestigiis daemonum*, trans. John Shea, *Witches, Devils, and Doctors in the
   Renaissance* (Binghamton, NY: Medieval & Renaissance Texts & Studies,
   1991), 180–181. One of Weyer's arguments against witch-hunting was
   that using women as his servants would be counter-productive to the
   Devil's evil purposes: 'because of their age and sex and as a result of the
   cold, moist, dense, sluggish constitution which renders their bodies
   unsuitable, they hinder the work of the demon's fine and subtle substance,
   so that if he seeks the cooperation of these women, he is disturbed and hin-
   dered in the performance of his task.' *Ibid.*, 85–86.
59 Clark, *Thinking With Demons*, 114.
60 *Ibid.*, 115.
61 See also Eliane Camerlynck, 'Fémininité et sorcellerie'; Sophie Houdard,
   Les Sciences du diable; Gerhild Scholz Williams, *Defining Dominion*.
62 Many of the arguments are borrowed almost verbatim from Nider.

63 Schnyder, I.6, p. 41: 'quia prone sunt ad credendum. et quia principaliter demon querit corrumpere fidem. ideo potius eas aggreditur'. This passage is supported by a reference to Ecclesiastes 19: 'Quia cito credit leuis esse corde et minorabitur.'

64 *Ibid.*, 'a natura propter fluxibilitatem complexionis facilioris sunt impressionis'.

65 *Ibid.*, p. 42. 'Mul[i]eres ferme vt pueri leui sententia sunt' – a paraphrase of a line by Terence.

66 *Ibid.* 'Mala ergo mulier ex natura cum citius in fide dubitat etiam citius fidem abnegat'.

67 *Ibid.*, p. 43: 'ex inordinatis affectionibus et passionibus varias vindictas querunt excogitant et infligunt siue per maleficia siue aliis quibuscumque mediis.'

68 *Ibid.*, 'Quantus insuper defectus in memoratiua potentia cum hoc sit in eis ex natura vitium nolle regi sed suos sequi impetus sine quacunque pietate ad hoc studet et cuncta memorata disponit.'

69 Summers, 47. Schnyder, I.6, 45. 'Omnia per carnalem concupiscientiam, que quia in eis est insatiabilis'.

70 Schnyder, I.6, 42.

71 *Ibid.*

72 See e.g. Margaret Y. MacDonald, *Early Christian Women and Pagan Opinion: The Power of the Hysterical Woman* (Cambridge: Cambridge University Press, 1996).

73 Graf, *Magic in the Ancient World*, 1.

74 Valerie I.J. Flint, 'The demonisation of magic and sorcery in late antiquity: Christian redefinitions of pagan religions', *Witchcraft and Magic in Europe: Ancient Greece and Rome*, 279–348: 279.

75 Kieckhefer, *Magic in the Middle Ages*, 38.

76 Clark, *Thinking With Demons*, 233. The intellectual history of natural and demonic magic is fascinating but well beyond the scope of this book. Part II of *Thinking With Demons* provides an excellent discussion of magic and its relationship to science. Kieckhefer's *Magic in the Middle Ages* is a useful introduction to the subject. His article 'The specific rationality of medieval magic' is a more complex analysis of magic in medieval culture. *American Historical Review* 99, 3 (June 1994): 813–836. See also Peters, *The Magician, The Witch, and the Law*; Flint, 'The demonisation of magic'; Richard Gordon, 'Imagining Greek and Roman magic', *Witchcraft and Magic in Europe: Ancient Greece and Rome*, 159–275; Ioan P. Couliano, *Eros and Magic in the Renaissance*, trans. Margaret Cook (Chicago and London: Chicago University Press, 1987; orig. *Eros et*

magie à la Renaissance, 1484, Paris, 1984); Elizabeth M. Butler, *Ritual Magic,* Magic in History (University Park, PA: Pennsylvania State University Press, 1998 [Cambridge: Cambridge University Press, 1949]); Noel L. Brann, *Trithemius and Magical Theology: A Chapter in the Controversy over Occult Studies in Early Modern Europe* (Albany: SUNY Press, 1999); D.P. Walker, *Spiritual and Demonic Magic from Ficino to Campanella,* Magic in History (University Park, PA: Pennsylvania State University Press, 2000; orig. pub. as vol. 22 of Studies of the Warburg Institute, The Warburg Institute, University of London, 1958).

77 Schnyder, I.2, 18. 'Concludamus quod ad maleficiales effectus de quibus ad presens loquimur malefici cum demonibus semper concurrere et vnum sine altero nihil posse efficere.' (We conclude that so far as the evil deeds of which we are now speaking are concerned, witches [male] always work with demons and one cannot make anything happen without the other.)

78 2.8, 116: 'sans la paction auec Sathan, quand vn homme auroit toutes les poudres, caracteres, & parolles des Sorcieres, il ne sçauroit faire mourir ny homme ny beste.'

79 E.g. Bodin, 1.3, 20: 'Agrippa ... a esté toute sa vie le plus grand Sorcier qui fut de son temps'. (Agrippa ... was for his whole life the greatest witch who existed in his time.) de Lancre, 1.2, 69: 'Ce grand Sorcier Agrippa était de cet avis'. (The great witch Agrippa was of this opinion.)

80 Augustine, *The City of God,* 8.17, 337–338.

81 Bodin, 1.3, 15: 'les malins esprits anciennement trompoient, comme ils font encores à present, en deux sortes l'vne ouuertement, auec pactions expresses, où il n'y auoit quasi que les plus lourdaux, & les femmes qui y fussent prises: l'autre sorte estoit pour abuser les hommes vertueux, & bien nais, par idolatrie, & soubs voile de religion'.

82 *Ibid.,* Preface, unpaginated: 'pour la plupart sont gens du tout ignorans ou vieilles femmes'.

83 Bodin's comments are not isolated, but similarly explicit statements are rare. However, in our view, the logic of demonology, combined with the explicit rhetoric one does find, supports the reading of demonological texts as implicitly feminising male witches.

84 Our argument here is influenced by the metaphor of the 'Hesse-net', described by H.M. Collins as a network, or spider's web, of concepts that is 'mutually supporting since everything is linked to everything else' but is also susceptible to change: 'by virtue of the way that everything is connected, a change in one link might reverberate through the whole of the network.' 'The scientist in the network: A sociological resolution of the problem of inductive inference', *Changing Order: Replication and*

Induction in Scientific Practice (Chicago and London: Chicago University Press, 1992 [1985]), 129–157: 131. See also Rorty, 'Inquiry as recontextualization'.

85 Cornwall and Lindisfarne, 'Dislocating masculinity', 18.

86 Bodin, 3.3, 135: 'Mais pourquoy Sathan ne depart de ses tresors cachez en terre à ses esclaues?' (Why does Satan not give his treasures, hidden in the earth, to his slaves?) *Ibid.*, 137–138: 'quel malheur peut estre plus grand que le rendre esclaue de Sathan pour si peu de recompence en ce monde, & la damnation eternelle en lautre?' (what misfortune can be greater than to become Satan's slave for so little recompense in this world, and eternal damnation in the other?).

87 See, for example, Cornwall and Lindisfarne, 'Dislocating masculinity'; Trexler, *Sex and Conquest*. For a classic discussion of the social and cultural meaning of slavery, see Orlando Patterson, *Slavery and Social Death: A Comparative Study* (Cambridge and London: Harvard University Press, 1982). Brian Levack has hinted at an association between servility and feminisation, but in the context of distinguishing between male magicians and female witches: *The Witch-Hunt in Early Modern Europe*, 38. Levack's citation of James I and VI's *Daemonologie* to support his view that male magicians commanded the Devil while female witches served him is somewhat misleading. Levack quotes the statement that 'Witches ar servantes onelie, and slaues to the Devil; but the Necromanciers are his maisters and commanders' out of context. The statement is a characterisation of vulgar opinion, which, as the text explains, is only 'in a maner true'. Men may command the Devil, 'not by anie power that they can haue over him, but *ex pacto* allanerlie: whereby he oblices himself in some trifles to them, that he may on the other part obteine the fruition of their body & soule'. King James the First, *Daemonologie, in Forme of a Dialogue* [1597], ed. G.B. Harrison (New York: Barnes and Noble, 1966), 9.

88 As according to the confession of an early modern witch reported by E. William Monter, *European Witchcraft* (New York: Wiliey, 1969), 80–81: 'She had used the said little bones to manufacture hail; this she was wont to do once or twice a year … At last the hail was sent over the marsh towards Weissingen, doing great damage.'

89 Briggs, *Witches and Neighbors*, 88: 'Cows, pigs, goats and sheep were all potential targets for witches; these were the animals which were kept for meat, milk, hides and wool and can be assimilated to crops in general.'

90 See Roper, 'Witchcraft and fantasy', *Oedipus and the Devil*, 199–225.

91 See Emmanuel Le Roy Ladurie, *Jasmin's Witch: An Investigation into Witchcraft and Magic in South-west France during the Seventeenth*

Century, trans. Brian Pearce (London: G. Braziller, 1987) and Roper's intriguing piece 'Stealing manhood: Capitalism and magic in early modern Germany', *Oedipus and the Devil*, 125–144.

92 Especially by 'cunning-folk' – as in the Veneto, where witchcraft was almost entirely associated with cunning-folk, whose main pursuits were love magic and seeking buried treasure – activities that almost certainly pre-dated the ascendancy of the 'elaborated concept' of diabolical witch-craft. See Ruth Martin, *Witchcraft and the Inquisition in Venice 1550–1650*.

93 Francisco Bethencourt, 'Portugal: A scrupulous Inquisition', *Centres and Peripheries*, 403–422: 414: 'Curses are, among witches' crafts, the most feared by the common people.'

94 Jeffrey Burton Russell, *Witchcraft in the Middle Ages*, (Ithaca, NY: Cornell University Press, 1972).

95 Ginzburg, *Ecstasies*, summarised as 'Deciphering the Sabbath' in Ankarloo and Henningsen, eds., *Centres and Peripheries*, 121–137.

96 Robert Muchembled, 'Satanic myths and cultural reality', 153.

97 See James Estes, *Christian Magistrate and State Church: The Reforming Career of Johannes Brenz* (Toronto: Toronto University Press, 1982); Brenz's comments cited here from Briggs, *Witches and Neighbors*, 201.

98 Briggs, *Witches and Neighbors*, 22.

99 E.g., Pierre de Lancre, Jean Bodin: the former set the ratio of those accused of witchcraft at 10:1 (female: male); the latter, at 50:1!

100 Briggs, *Witches and Neighbors*, 321.

101 Heikkinen and Kervinen, 'Finland: The male domination', 322; and see chapter 1. Much the same is true for Estonia, where of the 193 defendants whose gender is known, 60 per cent were men. Madar, 'Estonia I: Werewolves and poisoners', 266.

102 Hastrup, 'Iceland: Sorcerers and paganism', 399.

103 Gustav Henningsen, *The Witches' Advocate: Basque Witchcraft and the Spanish Inquisition* (Reno: University of Nevada Press, 1980), 391.

104 Briggs, *Witches and Neighbors*, 263.

105 As Christina Larner has put it, witches were accused not because they were women 'but because they were witches': *Witchcraft and Religion: The Politics of Popular Belief*, ed. Alan Macfarlane (Oxford: Basil Blackwell, 1984), 56 and 87.

CONCLUSION AND AFTERWORD

Historical ethics

Very few practising scholars today, except for a thin crust of aged historians in certain senior common rooms, in retirement-optional American universities, and a few young fogies in very old-fashioned departments, mourn the demise of 'great-man' history of the sort that concentrated on public figures (usually, but not exclusively, men – one must imagine Queen Elizabeth I, Catherine the Great and Maria Theresa as 'great men'), assuming them to have been the proper objects of historical study due not merely to their position and influence, but due to their supposed status as the very motors of History. Whatever the manifold problems – political, ethnic, ideological, methodological, epistemological – inherent in that kind of history, it had the distinct ethical advantage of studying people who were, by any standard, including their own, in the public eye: people who acted, spoke and wrote for public consumption, and often enough, for posterity as well. Before historians thought to bother with the doings not of, say, Metternich, but of the people in the German-speaking world whose lives were touched and in some ways shaped by Metternich's policies and by the 'Congress system' that dominated Europe after 1815, there was little reason to worry that historians might face the kind of ethical questions and conflicts of interest that cultural anthropologists, ethnologists, sociologists and a host of other students of contemporary people and cultures must confront, and in respect of which they must – very properly – perform 'ethics reviews', obtain waivers and clearances, allow their writing to be vetted by representatives of those studied, and remain accountable in some way to their subjects. Social historians and, more recently, historians of culture, labour, gender, women, folk medicine and the like – historians of everyday people and their lives – have dodged exactly the same issues confronted by those who study living people by insisting, rather irrelevantly, on the deadness of historical subjects. They cannot, it is argued, with irrefutable but nonetheless faulty logic, sign waivers, review our descriptions of them and their motives, bring actions for libel, or defend themselves publicly. The incorrect conclusion often drawn from this line of reasoning is that historians have *carte blanche* in interpreting the traces of their subjects' lives, indeed even in speaking for them – or through them.

Yet human beings who are now dead surely possessed agency and voice just as our contemporaries do. Copyright laws, for instance, recognise this, at least for a few decades after one's death. We cannot, it is true, obtain signed forms from those we study granting permission to observe certain activities, read certain papers, and the like. It is all the more important, therefore, that we listen carefully to their self-understandings and self-described motivations before we import our categories into the past to study them. That we have a right to import our own questions to the past is, surely, beyond reasonable question: why else do we study history? But we must be much more careful than many practitioners of social-science-model historical research have been; and we must have the courage to say that even so celebrated, indeed, so sexy a book as Lyndal Roper's *Oedipus and the Devil* is, in places, simply wrong because it uses modernist theory (theory built to help 'correct' 'superseded' or 'toxic' cultural formations) to understand the pre-modern world and imports current understandings of psychosexual dynamics to what are, granted, potentially psychosexually charged situations, but which were played out for entirely different reasons quite sufficient to explain said situations. We have no objections to subtle and playful (Walter Ong[1]) interpellation of the materials in question with psychoanalytic or other 'modern' or even contemporary theories in order to tease out hidden possibilities, tensions, ideas, so long as the historian's primary tools for understanding the past are in some clear sense congruent with that past, and so long as the historian retains a clear idea of the relationship, and probably the hierarchy, between past self-understandings and our attempts to understand the past using models we import. Brad Gregory has argued that psychoanalytic and similar kinds of general theories are never useful for trying to sort out past individuals' motivations;[2] while we are a bit less sceptical, we would first want to see sources that licence some such use.

Granted: germs, class loyalties and so on probably existed before Pasteur and Marx, and historians have good reasons to think about how plague spread and why, and what the dynamics of the Wat Tyler, Bundschuh or Peasants' War were. We can as historians acknowledge their existence and try to study them without betraying our subjects; but we must also be sympathetically aware of notions of miasma and estates to make sense of what they were up to in their terms. The latter concern has come far too short in the mainstream practice of history these last sixty or so years.

Then there are the complex cross-cutting problems presented by cultural-political agendas that need certain modernist tropes to validate their ascendancy. Roper's feminist account of male–female relations benefits a great deal from the discovery/existence of an oppressive, patriarchal psychosexual dynamic of sado-masochism in witch trials; in the case of modern analyses of martyrdom, modernist views of religion benefit even more by reducing martyrdom to psychological and perhaps even sado-masochistic aberrance. This is not to insist that those things were never there in the past; but they are not there in the sources Roper used, nor in the ones we have used, nor in the voluminous materials on martyrdom Brad Gregory amassed and analysed in his book *Salvation at Stake*.

Summation

We began by posing several questions, which may be summed up, informally, as 'What are these male witches doing in these demonological texts?' and 'Why doesn't anyone talk about this?' Not every single question that arises in the course of a research project can be answered, and this volume leaves certain issues essentially untouched. We have attempted, however, to address what we believe are the most funda-mental questions.

Chapter 1 tackled the first of these, namely, why male witches are not more common subjects in witchcraft historiography. Specialists in early modern witchcraft are aware that it was not sex-specific, even among the most misogynist demonologists. Modern scholars of various ideological and methodological leanings have excluded male witches from witch-craft historiography by either ignoring or 'declassifying' them. This exclusion betrays the unreflexive nature of much witchcraft historiogra-phy, in which political/ideological agendas (not limited to feminist schol-ars) and a priori assumptions are permitted to predetermine how early modern evidence is read and what conclusions are drawn from it.

In the second chapter, we began the work of unpacking conven-tional wisdom about witchcraft and gender. First, we presented data, synthesised from other scholars' archival research, that showed wide variation in the proportion of male to female witches. This data consti-tuted part of a more general criticism of the way witchcraft historians use statistical information to mask regional diversity and present a mono-chromatic picture of witchcraft prosecution dynamics. Second, we pre-sented two case studies of male witches in Essex and Germany. These case studies demonstrate that many generalisations about male witches, derived from specific regional studies, are not in fact suitable for Europe-wide application. For instance, the common generalisation that men were accused of witchcraft because they were related to a female witch, with the implication that there is a direct causal relationship, looks very shaky when examined closely in specific contexts. The notion that men were accused of practising different types of magic than women also appears dubious, although worthy of further investigation. In short, simplistic portrayals of the relationship between gender and witchcraft in early modern Europe do not reflect the complex and untidy state of affairs that even the briefest overview reveals.

In the third chapter, we examined issues of agency and resistance with an eye to placing witches' own self-understandings and motivations,

APPENDIX

JOHANNES JUNIUS: BAMBERG'S FAMOUS MALE WITCH

Dated 24 July 1628
Johannes Junius, burgomaster of Bamberg[1]

Many hundred thousand times good night, my daughter Veronica so dear to my heart. Innocent I came to jail, innocent I was tortured, innocent I must die. For whoever comes to the house[2] either must become a witch[3] or be tortured for so long that he claims something pulled from his imagination, and, God have mercy, figures out something to say. I want to tell you how things have gone for me. When I was put to the question the first time, Doctor Braun, Doctor Kötzendörffer and the two foreign Doctors[4] were there ... Then Doctor Braun from Abtswerth asked me: 'Kinsman, how did you end up here?' I answered: 'Through lies, misfortune.' 'Listen, you' he said, 'you are a witch. Do you wish to confess it freely? If not, witnesses will be brought forward, along with the executioner.' I said 'I am no witch, I have a clean conscience in this matter, even if there were a thousand witnesses, so I am not at all worried, but I will gladly hear the witnesses.' Then the son of the chancellor [Dr Haan[5]] was brought in, and I asked him, 'Sir Doctor, what do you know of me? I have never had anything to do [with you?], neither for good nor for ill, at any time in my life.' Then he answered me, 'Sir Colleague, on account of the regional court [*Landgericht*].' 'I beg you, produce your witnesses.' 'I saw you when they held court.' 'Well, but how?' He did not know. So I asked the Commissioners to place him under oath and examine him properly. Doctor Braun said they would not do it 'as you would have it done, it is enough that he saw you.' 'Go on, Sir Doctor!', I said, 'So, sir, what kind of a witness is this? If things can be done this way, then you are no more certain [of the facts] than I or any other honest man. There was no questioning [of the witness].' Then the chancellor came, and said the same thing as his son, namely that he also had seen me, but he had not looked at my feet to see what I was. Then came Hopffens Else [an accused day-labourer[6]]. She claimed to have seen me dancing in the Hauptsmoor forest.[7] I asked her how she saw. She answered that she did not know. I appealed to my lords for God's sake, they heard that these were all poor witnesses, they should be sworn to an oath and properly questioned, but that was not to be; rather [they] said, I should confess voluntarily or the executioner would certainly force me to do so. I answered: 'I have never renounced God, and did not plan to do so, and God should mercifully prevent me from doing so. I would rather endure what I had to.' And then came – God in highest Heaven have mercy – the executioner, and put the thumbscrews on me, both hands bound together, so that the blood ran out at the nails and everywhere, so that for four weeks I could not use my hands, as you can see from the writing. So I put myself in the care of God in his five sacred wounds[8] and said, because this concerns God's honour and name, which I have never denied, therefore I will commend my innocence and all the tortures and harm to his five wounds and he will lessen my pain, so that I can endure such pain. Thereafter they first stripped me, bound my hands behind me, and drew me up in the torture. Then I thought heaven and earth were at an end; eight times did they draw me up and let me fall again, so that I suffered horrible agony. [In the margin, sideways:] Dear child, six witnesses have testified at the same time against me: the chancellor, his son, Neudecker, Zaner, Hoffmaisters Ursel and Hopffens Else, all falsely, through coercion as they all have told me, and begged me [to forgive them] for God's sake before their sentences were executed … they knew nothing but good and nice things about me. They were forced to say it, just as I myself would experience …[9] I can have no priest, take careful note of this letter.

[page 2]

And all this happened when I was utterly naked, as they had me undress completely. And when our Lord God came to my aid, I said to them: 'God forgive you for attacking an innocent man in this way, wanting to take not only his life and soul, but also his goods and possessions.' Doctor Braun said 'You are a rascal.' I said 'I am no rascal, nor any such man and am just as honest as you all are, but so long as things go this way, no honest man in Bamberg will be safe, you no more than I or anyone else.' The Doctor said he was not subject to diabolical temptations; I said 'Nor am I, but your false witnesses, they are the devils, as well as your vicious tortures. For you let no one go, not even if he withstands all tortures.' And this happened on Friday the 30th of June. I had to endure all the tortures with God's help. And I was unable to get dressed this whole time or use my hands without the other pain that I had to suffer innocently. When the executioner took me back to jail, he said to me: 'Sir, I beg you, for God's sake confess something, whether it be true or not. Invent something, for you cannot bear the torture which you shall suffer; and even if you bear it all, you still shall not escape, not even if you were a count, but one torture will follow another until you say you are a witch. Not before that will they let you go, as you may see by their trials, for one is just like another.' Then Georg came to me and said my Lord [Bishop Johann Georg II] wanted to set such an example with me that people would be amazed. The executioners had been saying this the whole time and wanted to torture me again, and he begged me for God's sake to think something up because even if I were entirely innocent, I would never go free; Candelgiesser, Neudecker and others said the same thing to me. So I made a plea, saying that I was in very bad shape, they should give me a day to think about it and send me a priest. They refused me a priest, but gave me the time to think. Now dearest daughter, can you imagine in what kind of danger I was and still am! I was supposed to say that I was a witch, though I am not, and I am supposed to renounce God for the first time, though I have never done so before. I worried myself sick day and night, and finally I hit upon a plan. I would not worry about it, as I had not been allowed to see a priest who could advise me whether I should think something up and say it. I would surely be better to say it with my mouth and with words, even though I had not really done it; and afterwards I would confess it to the priest, and let those answer for it who compel me to do it. Then I asked to see the Father Prior in the Dominican monastery, but was not allowed to see him. And then my statement, as follows, is entirely made up.

[page 3]
Now follows, dear child, the statement I made, such that I escaped the worst and hardest tortures, which I could not possibly have withstood any longer. Namely: when I had a commission from Rottweil in the year 1624 or 1625, I had to give the Doctor [the Imperial Court Advocate Lukas Schlee zu Rottweil[10]] 600 gulden for the commission [in my report for Rottweil?], and that I addressed many honest people who had been of assistance to me. That is all true. Now follows my statement which is pure lies, which I [would have?] had to say under questioning accompanied by even greater tortures, and for which I must die. After that, I said that I was walking in a depressed state in my field near the *Friedrichsbrunnen*, and sat down there, and a wild [young?] girl came to me and said: 'Sir, what are you doing, why are you so sad?' I answered that I did not know, so she came closer. As soon as that happened, she became a billy-goat and said to me: 'See, now you see with whom you are dealing.' It grabbed me by the throat and said 'You must be mine or I will kill you!' Then I said 'God save me from that!' So he disappeared and came back quickly, bringing two women and three men with him. I was to deny God, and I have confessed that I[11] did so; I was to deny God and the heavenly host, and I have confessed that I did so; I have confessed that he then baptised me and the two women were the sponsors; that he gave me a ducat, but that it turned out to be a shard.

Then, thinking that I had finished, but they sent the executioner to me, and [asked] where I had been to go dancing, and I did not know which way was up. I remembered that the chancellor, his son and

Hopffens Else had named the old court, the council chambers and the Hauptsmoor, as well as other things I heard them read out in such cases, and I named those same places as well. Then I was supposed to say what sort of people I had seen there. I said that I had not recognised them. 'You old rascal, must I set the executioner on you?' ... 'Wasn't the chancellor there?' I said yes. 'Who else?' I recognised no one, I said. 'So,' he said, 'take one street after the other in turn. First go out to the market and then back in again.' So I had to name a number of people, and then turned to the Lange Gasse. I recognised no one from there. But I had to name eight persons from there, then Zinckenwert, another person, and then onto the Upper Bridge and out to the George Gate on both sides. I said I didn't recognise anyone from there either. I was asked if I hadn't recognised someone from the castle, whoever it might be, I should say so without hesitation. And they asked me about all the streets in this way, and I neither wanted nor could say anything more. So they turned me over to the executioner, who was told to unclothe me, cut my hair off and put me on the rack.[12] 'This rascal knows someone in the market place, spends time with him every day, and refuses to name him.' Then they named Dietmeyer,[13] and I was forced to name him too. Then I was to say what sort of evil things I had done. I said nothing.

He expected something from me but because I would not do it, he struck me. 'Hoist the rascal up!' So I said that I had been told to kill my children, but instead I killed a horse. It didn't help. I said I had also taken a [consecrated] host and buried it. Once I said that, they left me in peace.

Now dear child, here you have all my confession and [the record of] my trial, for which I must die. And they are sheer lies and inventions, so help me God. For I was forced to say all this through fear of the torture that was threatened beyond what I had already endured. For they never leave off with the torture till one confesses something; no matter how pious he really is, he must be a witch. Nobody escapes, even if he is a count. And if God does not provide the means to bring things back into the clear light of day, all [our?] kin will be burnt. For each must first confess out loud things he does not know to be the truth about other people, just as I had to do. Now God in Heaven knows that I cannot do and do not know the slightest thing [about the activities with which he was charged]. Therefore I die innocent and as a martyr. Child, I know you are as pious as I am, such that you already have much pain and if I were to counsel you, you should take as much money and letters [of credit, of protection?] as you have and go on a pilgrimage for around half a year, or if you can get out of the diocese for a time, I suggest you do so until it becomes clear what turn things will take. Many honourable men and woman in Bamberg go to church and do their other business, have no knowledge of evil, have a good conscience, just as I have had until now, as you know … and nonetheless are taken to the witches' house [*Trudenhaus*]. As long as he has his voice,[14] he must go, whether it is just or not. Neudecker,[15] the chancellor's son, Candelgiesser, the daughter of Hofmeister Wolff[16] and Hopffens Else all have confessed against me, all at the same time. I was truly forced into it, just as many others are and will be unless God provides some remedy. Dear child, keep this letter hidden so that it does not circulate, otherwise I will be tortured so severely that it does not bear thinking about, and the jailers will be beheaded. That is how strictly it is forbidden. You can let cousin Stamer read this letter quickly and in confidence. He will keep it quiet. Dear child, give this man a Reichstaler … I have been writing this letter for many days. My hands are badly lamed, I have in fact been very badly injured. I beg you for the sake of the Last Judgement, keep this letter under careful watch and pray for me as your father for a true martyr after my death … But be sure you do not make this letter public. Have Anna Maria[17] pray for me as well. You may boldly swear on my behalf that I am no witch [*Trudner*, sorcerer] but a martyr, and thus I die in readiness [for judgement]. Good night, for your father Johannes Junius will never see you again. 24 July a[nn]o 1628.

These passages have been published in excerpts in a number of venues: the slightly abridged text that we have translated was published in its

original orthography by Friedrich Leitschuh in 1883; an English translation was published by George Lincoln Burr in a pamphlet titled *The
Witch-Persecutions*,[18] another German version was printed by Soldan,
Heppe and Bauer in their polemical *Geschichte der Hexenprozesse* of
1911–12;[19] and a German version in modernised orthography and
form was published by Wolfgang Behringer in German.[20] A rather
stilted and highly abridged translation drawn from Burr's was published by Alan Kors and Edward Peters in 1972.[21]

Notes

1 Johannes Junius was, according to Friedrich Leitschuh, *Beiträge zur
   Geschichte des Hexenwesens*, born in 1573 in Niderweisach in the
   Wetterau. The Freiherr von Horn wrote, in a report that was in 1883 in
   the possession of Freiherr Emil von Marschalk, that Junius was a
   Bamberg city councillor (*Ratsherr*) from 1608 to 1613, mayor or burgomaster in 1614, city councillor again in 1615–16, burgomaster again
   from 1617, councillor in 1618–20, burgomaster 1621, councillor
   1622–23, and burgomaster 1624–28. This letter, edited (in part) by
   Leitschuh, was in the Royal Library at Bamberg. Many other city coun-
   cillors and five other Bamberg mayors, along with the bishop's chancellor, Dr Georg Adam Haan (and his entire family), were also executed for
   witchcraft (48).

2 The Bamberg witch-house, specially erected during the peak of the panic
   in 1627. See figure 2, taken from the illustration in Soldan and Heppe,
   Hexenprozesse, vol. 2, between pages 2 and 3, and adapted by George
   Frost, whom the authors would like to thank.

3 *Drudner* a Bavarian word (also *Trudner*) for sorcerer, witch.

4 According to a footnote in Friedrich Leitschuh's edition of the letter, pages
   49–55 (*Hexenwesen*), these were Doctors of Canon and Civil Law,
   Schwartzcontz and Herrnberger: 49 n. 2.

5 Leitschuh, *Hexenwesen*, 49 n. 3.

6 *Ibid.*, 50 n. 2.

7 A sandy-soil forest near Bamberg, known for its special species of pine,
   the *Hauptsmoorkiefer*; now a 'municipal forest' which until the second
   World War reached all the way to the main railway station; not a putative
   'Haupts-moor', as Burr as well as Kors and Peters render it. This forest
   is correctly identified by Leitschuh, *Hexenwesen*, 50 n. 3 and by Soldan

and Heppe, *Hexenprozesse*, vol. 2, 7. See details in a description of the environment in the Bamberg area at www.bnv_bamberg.de/home/ba0699/essays/heimat. htm

8 Referring to Jesus' wounds incurred during his crucifixion.

9 Cf. the incorrect translation in Kors and Peters, *Witchcraft in Europe 1100–1700*, 259: 'just as I myself was'; this is *reported speech* set *before* his torture.

10 Soldan's note, *Hexenprozesse*, vol. 2, 9.

11 The original is in the subjunctive of reported speech: Junius is reporting that he confessed to the judges that he denied God.

12 uf die Tortur zieh[en]'.

13 According to Soldan's note (p. 7), a distinguished and accomplished civil servant.

14 'Wenn er nur seine Stimme hat': Soldan also marks this obscure passage with a question mark (p. 12).

15 According to Leitschuh, this was doubtless the burgomaster Georg Neudecker, who was one of the four burgomasters of Bamberg uninterruptedly from 1612 to his arrest on 28 April 1628: *Hexenwesen*, 54 n. 1.

16 The daughter of the Prince-Bishop's *Zahlmeister* (paymaster, treasurer) Wolfgang Hofmeister, named Ursula: Leitschuh, *Hexenwesen*, 54 n. 2.

17 Anna Maria was Junius' daughter, a nun in the cloister of the Holy Sepulchre at Bamberg: Leitschuh, *Hexenwesen*, 55 n. 1.

18 *Translations and Reprints from the Original Sources of European History*, vol. 3 no. 4 (Philadelphia: n.p., 1897). Burr's version of Junius' letter is on pp. 23–28.

19 Soldan and Heppe, *Hexenprozesse*, vol. 2: Junius' letter to his daughter in German (original orthography) and a facsimile of the first sheet, 6–12.

20 Behringer, *Hexen und Hexenprozesse*, 305–310.

21 Kors and Peters, *Witchcraft in Europe 1100–1700*.

BIBLIOGRAPHY

Multiple editions of the same text are listed in chronological order, with pre-modern printings listed before modern reprintings. In order to distinguish between multiple copies of the same edition, listings of pre-modern editions include the libraries at which they are held and their catalogue numbers.

Primary sources

Anon., 'Sexual spells', *Ancient Christian Magic: Coptic Texts of Ritual Power*. Ed. Marvin W. Meyer and Richard Smith. Princeton: Princeton University Press, 1999. pp. 147–181.

Augustine. *The City of God against the Pagans*. Ed. and trans. R.W. Dyson. Cambridge Texts in the History of Political Thought. Cambridge: Cambridge University Press, 1998.

Binsfeld, Petrus. *Tractatus de confessionibus maleficorum et sagarum recognitus et auctus*. Trier, 1591. Houghton Library 24244.48.

Bodin, Jean. *De la demonomanie des sorciers*. Paris 1580, fac. edn. Hildesheim: Georg Olms, 1988.

——. *On the Demon-Mania of Witches*. Trans. Randy A. Scott, abr. and introd. Jonathan L. Pearl, Toronto: Centre for Reformation and Renaissance Studies, 1995.

Boyer, Paul and Stephen Nissenbaum, eds. *Salem-Village Witchcraft: A Documentary Record of Local Conflict in Colonial New England*. Boston: Northeastern University Press, 1993 [1972].

Burchard of Worms. *Decretum* Bk. X *(De incantatoribus et auguribus)*. *Patrologia Latina* 140, 831–854. Ed. J.-P. Migne. Paris: n.d.

Cockburn, J.S., ed. *Calendar of Assize Records: Essex Indictments, Elizabeth I.* London: HMSO, 1978.

Danaeus [Daneau], Lambertus. *De veneficis.* Frankfurt/Main, 1581. Houghton Library 24244.172.

de Lancre, Pierre. *Tableau de L'Inconstance des Mauvais Anges,* Paris 1613, abridged repr. Nicole Jacques-Chaquin, ed. Paris: Aubier, 1982.

Del Rio, Martin. *Investigations Into Magic.* Ed. And trans. P.G. Maxwell-Stuart. Manchester and New York: Manchester University Press, 2000.

Ewen, C. L'Estrange, ed. *Witch Hunting and Witch Trials: The Indictments for Witchcraft from the Records of 1373 Assizes held for the Home Circuit A.D. 1559–1736.* New York: Dial, 1929.

Gregory of Tours. *The History of the Franks.* Trans. Lewis Thorpe. Harmondsworth: Penguin, 1985 [1974].

Guazzo, Francesco Maria. *Compendium maleficarum* [Milan, 1608]. Ed. Montague Summers, trans. E.A. Ashwin, New York: Dover, 1988 [London: John Rodker, 1929].

Institoris, Heinrich and Jacob Sprenger. *Malleus maleficarum.* 1485? British Library IB 8581. [Almost certainly Speyer, 1487.]

——. *Malleus maleficarum.* Speyer: Drach, 1487. Houghton Library Inc. 2367.5.

——. *Malleus maleficarum. c.* 1490. British Library IB 8615.

——. *Malleus maleficarum.* 1492? British Library IA 8634.

——. *Malleus maleficarum.* Cologne, 1494. Houghton Library Inc. 1462.

——. *Malleus maleficarum.* Nuremberg, 1494. Houghton Library Inc. 2090 (16.3).

——. *Malleus maleficarum.* 1494. British Library IA 7468.

——. *Malleus maleficarum.* 1496. British Library IA 7503.

——. *Malleus maleficarum.* 1510? British Library 1606/312.

——. *Malleus maleficarum.* Cologne, 1511. British Library 719.b.1.

——. *Malleus maleficarum.* Cologne, 1520. British Library 719.b.2.

——. *Malleus maleficarum.* 1576. British Library 232A37.

——. *Malleus maleficarum*. 1580. British Library 718.c.48.

——. *Malleus maleficarum*. 1582. British Library 719.b.5.

——. *Malleus maleficarum*. Frankfurt, 1588. Houghton Library Inc. 24244.13.3.5.

——. *Malleus maleficarum*. 1600. British Library 719.b.3.

——. *Malleus maleficarum. Malleus maleficarum* vol. I. Lyons: Bourgeat, 1669. Bruce Peel Special Collections, University of Alberta, BF 1569 I59 I669.

——. *Malleus maleficarum. Malleus maleficarum* vol. I. Lyons: Bourgeat, 1669. British Library 719.1.18.

——. *Malleus maleficarum*. N.d. British Library IB 1953.

——. *Malleus maleficarum*. N.d. British Library 1606/345.

——. *Malleus maleficarum*. Speyer: Drach, 1487, fac. edn. Ed. André Schnyder. Göppingen: Kümmerle, 1991.

Isidore of Seville. *Etymologiae* Bk. VIII, Ch. IX *(De magis). Patrologia Latina* 82, 310–314. Ed. J.-P. Migne. Paris: n.d.

Jacquier, Nicolaus. *Flagellum haereticorum fascinariorum*. Frankfurt/ Main, 1581. Houghton Library 24244.172.

King James the First. *Daemonologie, in Forme of a Dialogue*, a work claimed by James I and VI. Edinburgh: Robert Walde-Grave, 1597 [repr. New York: Barnes and Noble, 1966].

Maurus, Rabanus. *De magicis artibus. Patrologia Latina* 110, 1095–1110. Ed. J.-P. Migne. Paris: n.d.

Molitor, Ulrich. *De laniis & phitonicis mulieribus*. Cologne, 1489, fac. edn. with French trans. Paris: Emile Nourry, 1926.

Nider, Ioannis. *Formicarius. Malleus maleficarum* vol. I. Lyons: Bourgeat, 1669. Bruce Peel Special Collections, University of Alberta, BF 1569 I59 1669.

——. [Nyder, Johannes] *Formicarius*. Köln, 1480, fac. edn.; introd. by Hans Biedermann. Graz: Akademischer Druck und Verlagsanstalt, 1971.

Remigius [Rémy], Nicolaeus. *Daemonolatreiae Libri Tres*. Lyons, 1595. Houghton Library 24244.5.

Spee, Friedrich. *Cautio criminalis*. Frankfurt, 1632, repr. Ed. Theo G.M. Van Oorschot. Tübingen and Basel: A. Franck, 1992.

Summers, Montague, trans. *The Malleus Maleficarum of Heinrich Kramer and James Sprenger*. New York: Dover, 1971 [London: John Rodker, 1928; repr. 1948].

Weyer, Johann. *De praestigiis daemonum*. Trans. John Shea. *Witches, Devils, and Doctors in the Renaissance*. Binghamton, NY: Medieval and Renaissance Texts and Studies, 1991.

Secondary sources

Ammann, Hartmann. 'Eine Vorarbeit des Heinrich Institoris für den *Malleus Maleficarum*'. *Mitteilungen des Instituts für Österreichische Geschichtsforschung*, suppl. vol. VIII. Ed. Oswald Redlich. Innsbruck: Wagner'sche Universitäts-Buchhandlung, 1911. pp. 461–504.

Amussen, Susan Dewar. *An Ordered Society: Gender and Class in Early Modern England*. Oxford: Blackwell, 1988.

Anglo, Sydney, ed. *The Damned Art: Essays in the Literature of Witchcraft*. London: Routledge & Kegan Paul, 1977.

Archer, Margaret S. *Being Human: The Problem of Agency*. Cambridge: Cambridge University Press, 2000.

Baroja, Julio Caro. *The World of the Witches*. Trans. Nigel Glendinning. London: Phoenix, 2001. Orig. *Las Brujas y su Mundo*. Madrid, 1961.

Barstow, Anne Llewellyn. *Witchcraze: A New History of the European Witch Hunts*. San Francisco: Pandora, 1995 [1994].

Barthes, Roland. 'The discourse of history'. *The Postmodern History Reader*. Ed. Keith Jenkins. London and New York: Routledge, 1997. pp. 120–123.

Bartov, Omer. 'German soldiers and the Holocaust: Historiography, research and implications'. *The Holocaust: Origins, Implementation, Aftermath*. Ed. Omer Bartov. London and New York: Routledge, 2000. pp. 162–184.

Baxter, Christopher. 'Johann Weyer's *De Praestigiis Daemonum*: Unsystematic psychopathology'. *The Damned Art: Essays in the Literature of Witchcraft*. Ed. Sydney Anglo. London: Routledge & Kegan Paul, 1977. pp. 53–75.

Behringer, Wolfgang. *Witchcraft Persecutions in Bavaria: Popular Magic, Religious Zealotry and Reason of State in Early Modern Europe*. Trans. J.C. Grayson and David Lederer. Cambridge: Cambridge University Press, 1997. Orig. *Hexenverfolgung in Bayern: Volksmagie, Glaubenseifer und Staatsräson in der Frühen Neuzeit*. Munich, 1987.

——. ed. *Hexen und Hexenprozesse*. Munich: dtv, 1988.

——. *Shaman of Oberstdorf: Chonrad Stoeckhlin and the Phantoms of the Night*. Trans. H.C. Erik Midelfort. Charlottesville, VA: Virginia University Press, 1998. Orig. *Chonrad Stoeckhlin und die Nachtschar: eine Geschichte aus der frühen Neuzeit*. Munich, 1994.

——. 'Witchcraft studies in Austria, Germany and Switzerland', *Witchcraft in Early Modern Europe. Studies in Culture and Belief*. Eds. Jonathan Barry, Marianne Hester and Gareth Roberts. Cambridge: Cambridge University Press, 1998 [1996]. pp. 64–95.

Berger, Maurice, Brian Wallis and Simon Watson eds. *Constructing Masculinity*. New York and London: Routledge, 1995.

Bethencourt, Francisco. 'Portugal: A scrupulous Inquisition'. *Early Modern European Witchcraft: Centres and Peripheries*. Eds. Bengt Ankarloo and Gustav Henningsen. Oxford: Clarendon, 1990. pp. 403–422.

Biddick, Kathleen. 'The Devil's anal eye: Inquisitorial optics and ethnographic authority'. *The Shock of Medievalism*. Durham and London: Duke University Press, 1998. pp. 105–134.

Bostridge, Ian. *Witchcraft and its Transformations, c. 1650–c. 1750*. Oxford: Clarendon, 1997.

Boyer, Paul and Stephen Nissenbaum. *Salem Possessed: The Social Origins of Witchcraft*. Cambridge, MA and London: Harvard University Press, 1996 [1974].

Brann, Noel L. *Trithemius and Magical Theology: A Chapter in the Controversy over Occult Studies in Early Modern Europe*. Albany: SUNY Press, 1999.

Brauner, Sigrid. *Fearless Wives and Frightened Shrews: The Construction of the Witch in Early Modern Germany*. Ed. Robert H. Brown. Amherst: Massachusetts University Press, 1995.

Briggs, Robin. *Witches and Neighbors: The Social and Cultural Context of European Witchcraft*. New York: Penguin, 1998 [Harper-Collins, 1996].

——. '"Many reasons why": Witchcraft and the problem of multiple explanation'. *Witchcraft in Early Modern Europe: Studies in Culture and Belief*. Eds. Jonathan Barry, Marianne Hester and Gareth Roberts. Cambridge: Cambridge University Press, 1998 [1996]. pp. 49–63.

Brod, Harry, ed. *The Making of Masculinities: The New Men's Studies*. Boston: Allen & Unwin, 1987.

Brown, Kathleen. *Good Wives, Nasty Wenches and Anxious Patriarchs*. Chapel Hill and London: University of North Carolina Press, 1996.

Burghartz, Susanna. 'The equation of women and witches: A case study of witchcraft trials in Lucerne and Lausanne in the fifteenth and sixteenth centuries'. *The German Underworld: Deviants and Outcasts in German History*. Ed. Richard J. Evans. London and New York: Routledge, 1988. pp. 57–74.

Burr, George Lincoln. *The Witch-Persecutions*. Translations and Reprints from the Original Sources of European History. Vol. 3, no. 4. Philadelphia: n.p., 1897.

Butler, Elizabeth M. *Ritual Magic*. Magic in History. University Park, PA: Pennsylvania State University Press, 1998 [Cambridge: Cambridge University Press, 1949].

Bynum, Caroline Walker. *Fragmentation and Redemption: Essays on Gender and the Human Body in Medieval Religion*. New York: Zone, 1992.

Cadden, Joan. *Meanings of Sex Difference in the Middle Ages: Medicine, Science, and Culture*. Cambridge: Cambridge University Press, 1995 [1993].

Camerlynck, Eliane. 'Fémininité et sorcellerie chez les théoriciens de la démonologie à la fin du Moyen Age: Étude du *Malleus maleficarum*'. *Renaissance and Reformation* 19 (1983): 13–25.

Clark, Stuart. *Thinking With Demons: The Idea of Witchcraft in Early Modern Europe*. Oxford: Clarendon, 1999 [1997].

——, ed. *Languages of Witchcraft: Narrative, Ideology and Meaning in Early Modern Culture*. Houndmills: Macmillan, 2001; New York: St Martin's, 2001.

Classen, Constance. *The Color of Angels: Cosmology, Gender and the Aesthetic Imagination*. London and New York: Routledge, 1998.

Cohen, Ira. 'Structuration theory and social *praxis*'. *Social Theory Today*. Eds. Anthony Giddens and Jonathan Turner. Stanford: Stanford University Press, 1987, 273–308.

Cohn, Norman. *Europe's Inner Demons: The Demonization of Christians in Medieval Christendom*. Rev. edn. London: Pimlico, 1993 [Chatto and Heinemann, 1975].

Collins, H.M. *Changing Order: Replication and Induction in Scientific Practice*. Chicago and London: Chicago University Press, 1992 [1985].

Compact Edition of the Oxford English Dictionary. Oxford: Oxford University Press, 1971.

Concise Oxford Dictionary of Current English. 9th edn. Ed. Della Thompson. Oxford: Clarendon, 1995.

Copelon, Rhonda. 'Surfacing gender: Reconceptualizing crimes against women in time of war'. *The Women and War Reader*. Eds. Lois Ann Lorentzen and Jennifer Turpin. New York and London: New York University Press, 1998. pp. 63–79.

Cornwall, Andrea and Nancy Lindisfarne. 'Dislocating masculinity: Gender, power and anthropology'. *Dislocating Masculinity:*

Comparative Ethnographies. Eds. Andrea Cornwall and Nancy Lindisfarne. London: Routledge, 1994. pp. 11–47.

Couliano, Ioan P. *Eros and Magic in the Renaissance.* Trans. Margaret Cook. Chicago and London: Chicago University Press, 1987. Orig. *Eros et magie à la Renaissance, 1484.* Paris, 1984.

Crelinsten, Ronald D. and Alex P. Schmid, eds. *The Politics of Pain: Torturers and their Masters.* Boulder, CO: Westview, 1995.

Cunningham, Andrew. 'Getting the game right: Some plain words on the identity and invention of science'. *Studies in the History and Philosophy of Science* 19 (1988): 382–383.

Davidson, Jane P. 'Great black goats and evil little women: The image of the witch in sixteenth-century German art'. *Journal of the Rocky Mountain Medieval and Renaissance Association* 6 (1985): 141–157.

Davies, Owen. *Witchcraft, Magic and Culture 1736–1951.* Manchester and New York: Manchester University Press, 1999.

de Blécourt, Willem. 'On the continuation of witchcraft'. *Witchcraft in Early Modern Europe. Studies in Culture and Belief.* Eds. Jonathan Barry, Marianne Hester and Gareth Roberts. Cambridge: Cambridge University Press, 1998 [1996]. pp. 335–352.

——. 'The witch, her victim, the unwitcher and the researcher: The continued existence of traditional witchcraft'. *Witchcraft and Magic in Europe: The Twentieth Century.* Eds. Bengt Ankarloo and Stuart Clark. Philadelphia: University of Pennsylvania Press, 1999; London: Athlone, 1999. pp. 141–219.

——. 'The making of the female witch: Reflections on witchcraft and gender in the early modern period'. *Gender and History* 12, 2 (2000): 287–309.

de Boer, Wietse. *The Conquest of the Soul: Confession, Discipline and Public Order in Counter-Reformation Milan.* Studies in Medieval and Reformation Thought 84. Leiden: Brill, 2001.

de Zulueta, Felicity. 'The torturers'. *A Glimpse of Hell: Reports on Torture Worldwide.* Ed. Duncan Forrest. New York: New York University Press, 1996. pp. 87–103.

Dolan, Frances E. *Dangerous Familiars: Representations of Domestic Crime in England 1550–1700*. Ithaca and London: Cornell University Press, 1994.

Dworkin, Andrea. *Woman-Hating*. New York: Dutton, 1974.

Ehrenreich, Barbara and Deirdre English. *Witches, Midwives and Nurses: A History of Women Healers*. Old Westbury, NY: Feminist Press, 1973; London: Writers and Readers Publishing Cooperative, 1973.

Estes, James. *Christian Magistrate and State Church: The Reforming Career of Johannes Brenz*. Toronto: University of Toronto Press, 1982.

Fanger, Claire, ed. *Conjuring Spirits: Texts and Traditions of Medieval Ritual Magic*. Magic in History. University Park, PA: Pennsylvania State University Press, 1998.

Faraone, Christopher A. *Ancient Greek Love Magic*. Cambridge and London: Harvard University Press, 1999.

Fisher, John Martin. *The Metaphysics of Free Will: An Essay on Control*. Cambridge: Blackwell, 1994.

Flint, Valerie I. J. *The Rise of Magic in Early Medieval Europe*. Princeton, NJ: Princeton University Press, 1994 [1991].

——. 'The demonisation of magic and sorcery in late antiquity: Christian redefinitions of pagan religions'. *Witchcraft and Magic in Europe: Ancient Greece and Rome*. Eds. Bengt Ankarloo and Stuart Clark. Philadelphia: University of Pennsylvania Press, 1999; London: Athlone, 1999. pp. 279–348.

Forrest, Duncan. 'Methods of torture and its effects'. *A Glimpse of Hell: Reports on Torture Worldwide*. Ed. Duncan Forrest. New York: New York University Press, 1996. pp. 104–121.

Foucault, Michel. *Discipline and Punish: The Birth of the Prison*. Trans. Alan Sheridan. New York: Vintage, 1995. Orig. *Surveiller et punir. Naissance de la prison*. Paris, 1976.

Foyster, Elizabeth. *Manhood in Early Modern England: Honour, Sex and Marriage*. London and New York: Longman, 1999.

Friedländer, Saul. 'The extermination of the European Jews in histori-ography: Fifty years later'. *The Holocaust: Origins, Implemen-tation, Aftermath*. Ed. Omer Bartov. London and New York: Routledge, 2000. pp. 79–91.

Gaskill, Malcolm. 'The Devil in the shape of a man: Witchcraft, conflict and belief in Jacobean England'. *Historical Research* 71, no. 175 (1988): 142–178.

Gehm, Britta. *Die Hexenverfolgungen im Hochstift Bamberg und das Eingreifen des Reichshofrates zu ihrer Beendigung*. Hildesheim: Georg Olm, 2000.

Gibson, Marion. *Reading Witchcraft: Stories of Early English Witches*. London and New York: Routledge, 1999.

Gijswijt-Hofstra, Marijke. 'Witchcraft before Zeeland magistrates and church councils, sixteenth to twentieth centuries'. *Witchcraft in the Netherlands from the Fourteenth to the Twentieth Century*. Eds. Marijke Gijswijt-Hofstra and Willem Frijhoff. Trans. Rachel M.J. van der Wilden-Fall. Rotterdam: Rotterdam University Press, 1991 [1987]. pp. 103–111.

——. 'Witchcraft after the witch-trials'. *Witchcraft and Magic in Europe: The Eighteenth and Nineteenth Centuries*. Eds. Bengt Ankarloo and Stuart Clark. Philadelphia: University of Pennsylvania Press, 1999. pp. 95–189.

Ginzburg, Carlo. *The Night Battles: Witchcraft and Agrarian Cults in the Sixteenth and Seventeenth Centuries*. Trans. John and Anne Tedeschi. London: Routledge and Kegan Paul, 1983. Orig. *I Benandanti: Stregoneria e culti agrari tra Cinquecento e Seicento*. Turin, 1966.

——. *Ecstasies: Deciphering the Witches' Sabbath*. Trans. Raymond Rosenthal. New York: Random House, 1991. Orig. *Storia Notturna*. Turin, 1989.

——. 'Deciphering the Sabbath'. *Early Modern European Witchcraft: Centres and Peripheries*. Eds. Bengt Ankarloo and Gustav Henningsen. Oxford: Clarendon, 1990. pp. 121–138.

Gordon, Richard. 'Imagining Greek and Roman magic'. *Witchcraft and Magic in Europe: Ancient Greece and Rome*. Eds. Bengt Ankarloo and Stuart Clark. Philadelphia: University of Pennsylvania, 1999; London: Athlone, 1999. pp. 159–275.

Govler, Sieglinde. 'Hexenwahr und Hexenprozesse in Kaernten von der Mitte des 15. bis zum ersten Drittel des 18. Jahrhunderts'. Diss. Graz 1955.

Graf, Fritz. *Magic in the Ancient World*. Trans. Franklin Philip. Cambridge, MA and London: Harvard University Press, 2000 [1997]. Orig. *Idéologie et Practique de la Magie dans l'Antiquité Gréco-Romaine*. Paris, 1994.

Gregory, Brad S. *Salvation at Stake: Christian Martyrdom in Early Modern Europe*. Cambridge, MA: Harvard University Press, 1999.

Harris, George W. *Agent-Centered Morality: An Aristotelian Alternative to Kantian Internalism*. Berkeley: University of California Press, 1999.

Hastrup, Kirsten. 'Iceland: Sorcerers and paganism'. *Early Modern European Witchcraft: Centres and Peripheries*. Eds. Bengt Ankarloo and Gustav Henningsen. Oxford: Clarendon, 1990. pp. 383–401.

Heikkinen, Antero and Timo Kervinen. 'Finland: The male domination'. *Early Modern European Witchcraft: Centres and Peripheries*. Eds. Bengt Ankarloo and Gustav Henningsen. Oxford: Oxford University Press, 1990. pp. 319–338.

Henningsen, Gustav. *The Witches' Advocate: Basque Witchcraft and the Spanish Inquisition*. Reno: University of Nevada Press, 1980.

——. '"The ladies from outside": An archaic pattern of the witches' Sabbath'. *Early Modern European Witchcraft: Centres and Perpheries*. Eds. Bengt Ankarloo and Gustav Henningsen. Oxford: Clarendon, 1990. pp. 191–215.

Hester, Marianne. *Lewd Women and Wicked Witches: A Study in the Dynamics of Male Domination*. London and New York: Routledge, 1992.

Hindle, Steve. 'The shaming of Margaret Knowsley: Gossip, gender and the experience of authority in early modern England'. *Continuity and Change* 9 (1994): 391–419.

Houdard, Sophie. *Les Sciences du diable: Quatre Discours sur la sorcellerie, Xve–XVIIe siècle*. Paris: Editions du Cerf, 1992.

Htet, Aung Moe, ed. *Tortured Voices: Personal Accounts of Burma's Interrogation Centers*. Bangkok: All Burma Students' Democratic Front, 1998.

Hutton, Ronald. *The Triumph of the Moon: A History of Modern Pagan Witchcraft*. Oxford: Oxford University Press, 1999.

Jempson, Mike. 'Torture worldwide'. *A Glimpse of Hell: Reports on Torture Worldwide*. Ed. Duncan Forrest. New York: New York University Press, 1996. pp. 46–86.

Jenkins, Keith. 'Introduction: On being open about our closures'. *The Postmodern History Reader*. Ed. Keith Jenkins. London and New York: Routledge, 1997. pp. 1–35.

Johns, Adrian. *The Nature of the Book: Print and Knowledge in the Making*. Chicago: Chicago University Press, 1998.

Kamber, P. 'La chasse aux sorciers et aux sorcières dans le Pays de Vaud'. *Revue Historique Vaudoise* 90. (1982): 21–33.

Karlsen, Carol F. *The Devil in the Shape of a Woman: Witchcraft in Colonial New England*. New York and London: W.W. Norton, 1987.

Kieckhefer, Richard. *European Witch Trials: Their Foundations in Popular and Learned Culture*. Berkeley: University of California, 1976.

——. 'The specific rationality of medieval magic'. *American Historical Review* 99, 3 (June 1994): 813–836.

——. *Magic in the Middle Ages*. Cambridge: Cambridge University Press, 1997 [1989].

——. *Forbidden Rites: A Necromancer's Manual of the Fifteenth Century*. Magic in History. University Park, PA: Pennsylvania State University Press, 1998 [Stroud: Sutton, 1997].

Klaits, Joseph. *Servants of Satan: The Age of the Witch Hunts.* Bloomington: Indiana University Press, 1985.

Klaniczay, Gabor. 'Hungary: The accusations and the universe of popular magic'. *Early Modern European Witchcraft: Centres and Peripheries.* Eds. Bengt Ankarloo and Gustav Henningsen. Oxford: Clarendon, 1990. pp. 219–255.

Klöse, Hans-Christian. 'Die angebliche Mitarbeit des Dominikaners Jakob Sprenger am Hexenhammer nach einem alten Abdinghofer Brief'. *Paderbornensis Ecclesia: Beiträge zur Geschichte des Erzbistums Paderborn, Festschrift für Lorenz Kardinal Jaeger zum 80. Geburtstag am 23. September 1972.* Ed. Paul-Werner Scheele. Munich: Ferdinand Schöningh, 1972. pp. 197–205.

Kors, Alan C. and Edward Peters, eds. *Witchcraft in Europe 1100–1700: A Documentary History.* Philadelphia: University of Pennsylvania Press, 1997 [1972].

Kramer, Heinrich (Institoris). *Der Hexenhammer. Malleus Maleficarum.* Trans. from the Latin by Wolfgang Behringer, Günter Jerouschek and Werner Tschacher, edited and introduced by Günter Jerouschek and Wolfgang Behringer. Munich: DTV, 2001 [2nd edn.].

Labouvie, Eva. 'Männer im Hexenprozess: Zur Sozialanthropologie eines "männlichen" Verständnisses von Magie und Hexerei'. *Geschichte und Gesellschaft* 16 (1990): 56–78.

La Fontaine, Jean. 'The history of the idea of Satan and Satanism'. *Witchcraft and Magic in Europe: The Twentieth Century.* Eds. Bengt Ankarloo and Stuart Clark. Philadelphia: University of Pennsylvania Press, 1999; London: Athlone, 1999. pp. 83–93.

Laqueur, Thomas. *Making Sex: Body and Gender from the Greeks to Freud.* Cambridge, MA: Harvard University Press, 1990.

Larner, Christina. *Enemies of God: The Witch Hunt in Scotland.* London: Chatto & Windus, 1981.

——. *Witchcraft and Religion: The Politics of Popular Belief.* Ed. Alan Macfarlane. Oxford: Basil Blackwell, 1984.

Leitschuh, Friedrich. *Beiträge zur Geschichte des Hexenwesens in Franken*. Bamberg: Hübscher, 1883.

Le Roy Ladurie, Emmanuel. *Jasmin's Witch: An Investigation into Witchcraft and Magic in South-west France during the Seventeenth Century*. Trans. Brian Pearce. London: G. Braziller, 1987.

Levack, Brian P. *The Witch-Hunt in Early Modern Europe*. 2nd edn. London and New York: Longman, 1995.

——. 'State building and witch hunting in early modern Europe'. *Witchcraft in Early Modern Europe: Studies in Culture and Belief*. Eds. Jonathan Barry, Marianne Hester and Gareth Roberts. Cambridge: Cambridge University Press, 1998 [1996]. pp. 96–115.

Lewis, Gilbert. 'Magic, religion and the rationality of belief', *Companion Encyclopedia of Anthropology*. Ed. Tim Ingold. London and New York: Routledge, 1994. pp. 563–590.

MacDonald, Margaret Y. *Early Christian Women and Pagan Opinion: The Power of the Hysterical Woman*. Cambridge: Cambridge University Press, 1996.

Macfarlane, Alan. *Witchcraft in Tudor and Stuart England: A Regional and Comparative Study*. Repr. Prospect Heights, IL: Waveland, 1991 [London: Routledge, 1970].

Madar, Maia. 'Estonia I: Werewolves and poisoners'. *Early Modern European Witchcraft: Centres and Peripheries*. Eds. Bengt Ankarloo and Gustav Henningsen. Oxford: Clarendon, 1990. pp. 257–272.

Martin, Ruth. *Witchcraft and the Inquisition in Venice 1550–1650*. Oxford: Basil Blackwell, 1989.

Michelet, Jules. *Satanism and Witchcraft: A Study in Medieval Superstition*. Trans. A.R. Allison. New York: Citadel, 1939. Orig. *La sorcière*. Paris, 1862.

Midelfort, H.C. Erik. *Witch Hunting in Southwestern Germany 1562–1684: The Social and Intellectual Foundations*. Stanford: Stanford University Press, 1972.

Monter, E. William. *European Witchcraft*. New York: Wiliey, 1969.

——. *Witchcraft in France and Switzerland: The Borderlands During the Reformation*. Ithaca and London: Cornell University Press, 1976.

——. 'Toads and eucharists: The male witches of Normandy, 1564–1660'. *French Historical Studies* 20, no. 4 (1997): 563–595.

Muchembled, Robert. 'Satanic myths and cultural reality'. *Early Modern European Witchcraft: Centres and Peripheries*. Eds. Bengt Ankarloo and Gustav Henningsen. Oxford: Clarendon, 1990. pp. 139–160.

Muir, Edward. *Ritual in Early Modern Europe*. Cambridge: Cambridge University Press, 1997.

Murray, Margaret. *The Witch-Cult in Western Europe*. London: Oxford University Press, 1921.

Naess, Hans Eyvind. 'Norway: The criminological context'. *Early Modern European Witchcraft: Centres and Peripheries*. Eds. Bengt Ankarloo and Gustav Henningsen. Oxford: Clarendon, 1990. pp. 367–382.

Oestmann, Peter. *Hexenprozesse am Reichskammergericht*. Cologne: Böhlau, 1997.

Ogden, Daniel. 'Binding spells: Curse tablets and voodoo dolls in the Greek and Roman worlds'. *Witchcraft and Magic in Europe: Ancient Greece and Rome*. Eds. Bengt Ankarloo and Stuart Clark. Philadelphia: University of Pennsylvania, 1999; London: Athlone, 1999. pp. 1–90.

Ong, Walter. *Fighting for Life: Contest, Sexuality, and Consciousness*. Ithaca, NY: Cornell University Press, 1981.

Patterson, Orlando. *Slavery and Social Death: A Comparative Study*. Cambridge and London: Harvard University Press, 1982.

Pearl, Jonathan. 'Witchcraft in New France in the seventeenth century: The social aspect'. *Historical Reflections/Réflexions Historiques* 4, no. 1 (1977): 191–205.

——. *The Crime of Crimes: Demonology and Politics in France 1520–1620*. Waterloo, Ont.: Wilfrid Laurier University Press, 1999.

Peters, Edward. *The Magician, the Witch, and the Law*. Philadelphia: University of Pennsylvania Press, 1992 [1978].

Pócs, Éva. *Between the Living and the Dead: A Perspective on Witches and Seers in the Early Modern Age*. Trans. Szilvia Rédey and Michael Webb. Budapest: Central European University Press, 1999. Orig. *Étok és holtak, látók és boszorkányok*, 1997.

Porter, Roy. 'Witchcraft and magic in enlightenment, romantic and liberal thought'. *Witchcraft and Magic in Europe: The Eighteenth and Nineteenth Centuries*. Eds. Bengt Ankarloo and Stuart Clark. Philadelphia: University of Pennsylvania Press, 1999. pp. 191–282.

Purkiss, Diane. *The Witch in History: Early Modern and Twentieth Century Representations*. London and New York: Routledge, 1996.

——. 'Desire and its deformities: Fantasies of witchcraft in the English Civil War', *Journal of Medieval and Early Modern Studies* 27, 1 (1997): 103–132.

Quaife, G.R. *Godly Zeal and Furious Rage: The Witch in Early Modern Europe*. New York: St Martin's, 1987.

Rapley, Robert. *A Case of Witchcraft: The Trial of Urbain Grandier*. Montreal and Kingston: McGill-Queen's University Press, 1998.

Reis, Elizabeth. *Damned Women: Sinners and Witches in Puritan New England*. Ithaca and London: Cornell University Press, 1999 [1997].

Renczes, Andrea. *Wie löscht man eine Familie aus? Eine Analyse Bamberger Hexenprozesse*. Pfaffenweiler: Centaurus-Verlagsgesellschaft, 1992.

Roper, Lyndal. *Oedipus and the Devil: Witchcraft, Sexuality and Religion in Early Modern Europe*. London and New York: Routledge, 1994.

Rorty, Richard. *Objectivity, Relativism, and Truth: Philosophical Papers Volume 1*. Cambridge: Cambridge University Press, 1997 [1991].

Rosaldo, Renato. 'After objectivism'. *The Cultural Studies Reader*. Ed. Simon During. London and New York: Routledge, 1993. pp. 104–117.

Rosenthal, Bernard. *Salem Story: Reading the Witch Trials of 1692*. Cambridge: Cambridge University Press, 1995 [1993].

Rowland, Robert. '"Fantasticall and Devilishe Persons": European witch-beliefs in comparative perspective'. *Early Modern European Witchcraft: Centres and Peripheries*. Eds. Bengt Ankarloo and Gustav Henningsen. Oxford: Clarendon, 1990. pp. 161–190.

Russell, Jeffrey Burton. *Witchcraft in the Middle Ages*. Ithaca, NY: Cornell University Press, 1972.

Ryan, W.F. *The Bathhouse at Midnight: A Historical Survey of Magic and Divination in Russia*. Magic in History. University Park, PA: Pennsylvania State University Press, 1999.

Scott, Joan Wallach. *Gender and the Politics of History*. New York: Columbia University Press, 1988.

Segl, Peter, ed. *Der Hexenhammer: Entstehung und Umfeld des* Malleus maleficarum *von 1487*. Cologne: Böhlau, 1988.

——. 'Heinrich Institoris. Persönlichkeit und literarisches Werk'. *Der Hexenhammer: Entstehung und Umfeld des* Malleus maleficarum *von 1487*. Ed. Peter Segl. Cologne: Böhlau, 1988.

Sharpe, James. *Instruments of Darkness: Witchcraft in England 1550–1750*. London: Penguin, 1997 [n.p.: Hamish Hamilton, 1996].

Silverman, Lisa. *Tortured Subjects: Pain, Truth, and the Body in Early Modern France*. Chicago and London: Chicago University Press, 2001.

Soldan, Wilhelm Gottlieb and Henriette Heppe. *Geschichte der Hexenprozesse*. New and rev. edn. by Max Bauer. 2 vols. Munich: Georg Müller, 1911–12.

Sörlin, Per. *'Wicked Arts': Witchcraft and Magic Trials in Southern Sweden, 1635–1754*. Leiden: Brill, 1999.

Stephens, Walter. *Demon Lovers: Witchcraft, Sex and the Crisis of Belief*. Chicago: Chicago University Press, 2002.

Strauss, Gerald. *Luther's House of Learning: Indoctrination of the Young in the German Reformation*. Baltimore: Johns Hopkins University Press, 1978.

Thomas, Keith. *Religion and the Decline of Magic: Studies in Popular Beliefs in Sixteenth and Seventeenth Century England*. Repr. London: Penguin, 1991 [Weidenfeld & Nicolson, 1971].

Trevor-Roper, H.R. *The European Witch-Craze of the Sixteenth and Seventeenth Centuries*. Repr. London: Penguin, 1990. Orig. pub. in *Religion, the Reformation and Social Change*, London: Macmillan, 1967.

Trexler, Richard C. *Sex and Conquest: Gendered Violence, Political Order, and the European Conquest of the Americas*. Ithaca, NY.: Cornell University Press, 1995.

Trumbach, Randolph. *Sex and the Gender Revolution*. Chicago: Chicago University Press, 1998.

Turner, James Grantham, ed. *Sexuality and Gender in Early Modern Europe: Institutions, Texts, Images*. Cambridge: Cambridge University Press, 1995.

Valentinitsch, H. 'Die Verfolgung von Hexen und Zauberern im Hertzogtum Steiermark – eine Zwischenbilanz'. *Hexen und Zauberer: Die grosse Verfolgung – ein europäisches Phänomen in der Steiermark*. Ed. H. Valentinitsch. Graz: n.p., 1987. pp. 297–316.

Veenstra, Jan R. *Magic and Divination at the Courts of Burgundy and France: Text and Context of Laurens Pignon's* Contre les devineurs *(1411)*. Leiden: Brill, 1998.

Walker, D.P. *Spiritual and Demonic Magic from Ficino to Campanella*. Magic in History. University Park, PA: Pennsylvania State University Press, 2000. Orig. pub. as vol. 22 of Studies of the Warburg Institute, The Warburg Institute, University of London, 1958.

Wiesner, Merry E. *Women and Gender in Early Modern Europe*. Cambridge: Cambridge University Press, 1995 [1993].

Williams, Gerhild Scholz. *Defining Dominion: The Discourses of Magic and Witchcraft in Early Modern France and Germany*. Ann Arbor: Michigan University Press, 1995.

Willis, Deborah. *Malevolent Nurture: Witch-Hunting and Maternal Power in Early Modern England*. Ithaca and London: Cornell University Press, 1995.

Wilson, Eric. 'The text and content of the *Malleus Maleficarum* (1487)'. Unpublished dissertation. Cambridge University, 1991.

Wittman, P. 'Die Bamberger Hexenjustiz 1595–1631'. *Archiv für das katholische Kirchenrecht* 50 (1883): 177–223.

Zika, Charles. 'Dürer's witch, riding woman and moral order'. *Dürer and his Culture*. Eds. Dagmar Eichberger and Charles Zika. Cambridge: Cambridge University Press, 1988. pp. 118–140.